PACIFIC MARINE FISHES

WARREN BURGESS & DR. HERBERT R. AXELROD

1. *Centropyge ferrugatus*, the rusty angelfish, which was discovered by Dr. John E. Randall in Ishigaki, Ryukyu Islands and which is described as a new species on page 21. This specimen, the type, is about $3\frac{1}{2}$ inches long. Photo by Dr. John E. Randall.

Book 1

SECOND EDITION ©1973 T. F. H. PUBLICATIONS, INC. LTD.

ISBN 0-87666-123-1

Distributed in the U.S.A. by T.F.H. Publications, Inc., 211 West Sylvania
Avenue, P.O. Box 27, Neptune City, N.J. 07753; in England by T.F.H.
(Gt. Britain) Ltd., 13 Nutley Lane, Reigate, Surrey; in Canada by Clarke,
Irwin & Company, Clarwin House, 791 St. Clair Avenue West, Toronto
10, Ontario; in Southeast Asia by Y. W. Ong, 9 Lorong 36 Geylang,
Singapore 14; in Australia and the south Pacific by Pet Imports Pty.
Ltd., P.O. Box 149, Brookvale 2100, N.S.W., Australia.
Published by T.F.H. Publications, Inc. Ltd., The British Crown Colony of
Hong Kong.

TABLE OF CONTENTS

INTRODUCTION

They say that the measure of a man might be how high he looks into the sky; others might call this same "far-sighted" individual a dreamer. Quite frankly we don't know what we are, but both of us have a burning desire to publish a book illustrating ALL the known coral fishes to be found in the Indo-Pacific Ocean . . . in color!!! There has never been an accurate count made of the Pacific coral fishes; as a matter of fact, there has never been an accurate count made of the known fishes of the world, but most experts agree that the figure lies around 20,000 species. We guess there are about 4,000 of these to be found in, on or near Pacific coral reefs.

For years both authors (HRA and WEB) have been collecting and photographing Pacific marine fishes; probably 40 years of research and work is represented in this series of books, of which this volume is the first.

Book I is basically a book about fishes of the western Pacific, primarily those found around the coral reefs of the Ryukyu Islands, and for this reason we have taken the photos from the basic work of two Japanese scientists, Dr. Yoshio Hiyama and Dr. Fujio Yasuda, prepared a new text, brought the nomenclature up to date, and presented it as our first volume, with about 400 species represented in color.

As we obtain sufficient material, we hope to add about one volume a year, until ten years hence, the entire project will be completed. Unfortunately, as the more common fishes fill the first volumes, the remaining species become more difficult to find. An international team of dedicated amateurs and professional ichthyologists will be assisting us in the collection, identification and photography of these remaining species.

Japanese coral fishes are to be found mainly around Ishigaki Island, and as the marine aquarium hobby in Japan keeps growing, more and more beautiful coral fishes will be collected and photographed for our future editions. The same is true of the Great Barrier Reef in Australia.

One of us (WEB) has spent many years studying the families Chaetodontidae and Pomacanthidae, the beautiful families which include the marine butterflyfishes and angelfishes, under the inspiring supervision of Dr. John Randall, working for a Doctor of Philosophy degree. As a result of this basic research we hope to be able to include photographs of almost all the known butterflyfishes; at least we'll have more color photographs in the first two volumes of this work than have ever appeared before . . . with several new species included as well!

This series of books is primarily dedicated to the presentation and proper identification of Pacific marine fishes. It is designed to be helpful to ichthyologists, divers, collectors, dealers, and aquarists, and the authors welcome correspondence with these groups to achieve a complete file of good quality color photographs, preferably Kodachromes, of fishes which are rare and difficult to find.

We have tried, wherever possible, to give the size of each fish illustrated in terms of standard length (the length measured from the tip of the snout to the base of the tail fin, without the tail fin itself), the exact source of the particular specimen illustrated, and its common and scientific name. For many of the species we invented a common name, since many of the fishes illustrated had never appeared in the popular literature before and thus had never been identified with a common name in English. It is possible, and even projected, that the same species might be illustrated several times in the forthcoming volumes as we obtain better photographs, or photographs which show geographical variations or color varieties of a given species.

The variety of fishes is almost limitless. In the following pages examples of the diversity of fish life of the Pacific Ocean are given. Among them are fishes outstanding for their beauty, and others for their ugliness. Some fishes are able to inflate themselves into the shape of a balloon, others can swim through the sand, and still others can change colors instantly so as to blend with their surroundings and virtually disappear. There are fishes equipped with 'rods' and 'bait' that angle for their dinner. And well known are the flying-fishes that can glide over the water's surface with outstretched wing-like fins.

The text includes information on the families of fishes illustrated. The captions give scientific name, size, area where it was captured or seen, and additional information about the fish such as common name, interesting habits, or distinctive characteristics. One thing all of the fishes in this book have in common is that they can be found in the Pacific Ocean. Many of them have wide distributions including the tropical areas of both the Pacific and Indian Oceans while others may be restricted in their range to an area such as southern Japan and vicinity.

The help we have received from Yoshio Hiyama, Fujio Yasuda, John Randall, Yasuhiko Taki, and Gerald Allen deserves a special note of thanks. Without them this first volume would have been much less accurate and extremely less colorful.

Herbert R. Axelrod

Warren E. Burgess

Family POMACANTHIDAE

ANGELFISHES

The brilliant colors and patterns of angelfishes have captured the attention of scientists and laymen alike. Their capacity to completely change color patterns as they transform from the juvenile stage to the adult has confused many people and has resulted in having several different names applied to each species. In the color plates of this book we have attempted to show several of these changes (some never before recorded), including the intermediate stages necessary to connect the adult and juvenile stages of these fishes. The smaller-sized angelfishes, members of the genera *Centropyge* and *Genicanthus,* do not exhibit these remarkable differences, although some species may undergo subtle changes.

The angelfishes have, until recently, been classified with the butterflyfishes. Scientific investigations carried out by one of the authors (WEB), however, have proved that they are different enough to be placed in separate families. For practical purposes all angelfishes can be distinguished from all butterflyfishes by the presence of a strong sharp spine on the lower edge of the preopercular bone of the angelfishes.

Angelfishes have small mouths set with rows of slender teeth, giving the appearance of a brush. The food of the angelfishes consists of small invertebrates, including such unusual items as sponges, coral polyps, and algae. Although no angelfish has an elongated snout for reaching normally inaccessible areas, such as is found in the butterflyfishes, they are able to maneuver quite easily and can eat difficult-to-reach items even though it means placing themselves in an upside-down position.

Most, if not all, of the angelfishes are tropical and occur only in warm, shallow ocean water where living reef corals are able to exist. Greater interest in SCUBA diving, underwater photography, and marine aquarium keeping has enabled us to present to you in this volume new photographs as well as previously unpublished information on the angelfishes.

Angelfishes vary in size from the small species of the genus *Centropyge,* attaining a length of three to four inches, to the larger species included in such genera as *Pomacanthus* and *Holacanthus,* growing to a length of two feet or more.

In nature and in captivity, angelfishes are territorial; that is, they select a particular area for their own and will defend it from all trespassers. In an aquarium two members of the same species will quarrel almost continuously, and these quarrels usually end in death for one of them. If one of the angelfishes is established in an aquarium, chances are it can defeat a new addition to the aquarium even though the newcomer is considerably larger than the original inhabitant.

Differences between the sexes of angelfishes are not known for more than a handful of species. The figures of *Genicanthus watanabei* show the differences between the male and the female of that species. Quite often, on the reef, angelfishes will be seen as pairs. It is still not known whether two such fish represent a male and a female, possibly a mated pair, or just an incidental association.

The distinctive color patterns of the angelfishes make identification relatively easy, so long as the species are properly identified in the available references. Even so, there is still some confusion between

2. *Pomacanthus imperator* (Bloch). Juvenile, 30 mm standard length. Okinawa. The young Emperor angelfish here will undergo very striking color changes as it grows to adulthood. This and the following eight photographs depict these changes as well as some of the variations encountered in this species. Family Pomacanthidae.

one or two species. Until recently, all small almost totally yellow angelfishes were quickly identified as the lemonpeel, *Centropyge flavissimus*. In 1953, another species of almost entirely yellow-colored angelfish, *Centropyge heraldi*, was described by Drs. Woods and Schultz. With two species now available, re-examination of the catches revealed that the two can easily be distinguished on the basis of color. The lemonpeel has a blue ring around the eye, along with other bright blue markings. *Centropyge heraldi*, or Herald's an-

gelfish, lacks the blue markings; instead it has a dark-bordered orange stripe in the anal fin. Another species, *Chaetodontoplus chrysocephalus*, the figure of which is the first ever to be published, was often confused with *Chaetodontoplus septentrionalis*. The color pattern of *Chaetodontoplus chrysocephalus* looks intermediate between that of *C. septentrionalis* and *C. melanosoma*. Although this does not necessarily mean it is a hybrid cross between these two species, it does indicate that they are closely related.

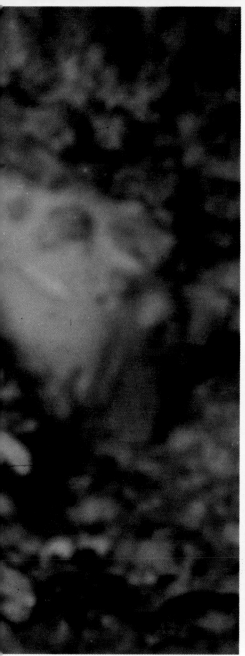

3. *Pomacanthus imperator* (Bloch). 40 mm standard length. Okinawa.

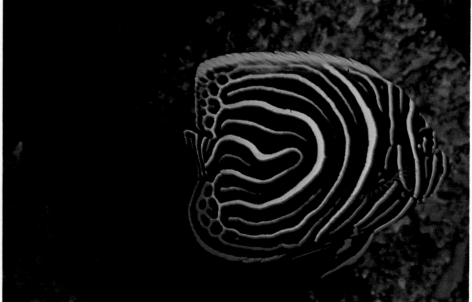

4. *Pomacanthus imperator* (Bloch). 50 mm standard length. Okinawa.

5. *Pomacanthus imperator* (Bloch). 50 mm standard length. Okinawa. Another example of the different patterns one might encounter in the juvenile Emperor angelfish.

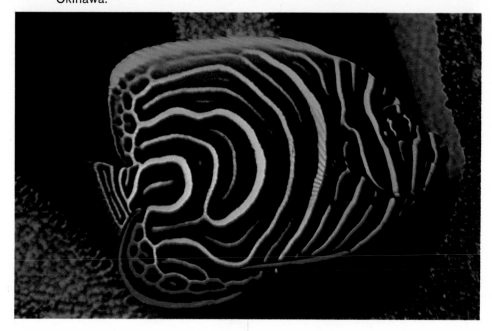

6. *Pomacanthus imperator* (Bloch). 50 mm standard length. Okinawa. The typical color pattern of the young Emperor angelfish. Note the complete white circle near the posterior end of the fish.

7. *Pomacanthus imperator* (Bloch). 70 mm standard length. Okinawa.

8. *Pomacanthus imperator* (Bloch). 100 mm standard length. Okinawa. The adult pattern is dominant in this fish but there are still faint traces of the circular pattern of the juveniles.

9. *Pomacanthus imperator* (Bloch). 120 mm standard length. Okinawa. Although no trace of the juvenile color pattern remain the adult pattern has not reached its final form.

Although color patterns are relatively uniform from one fish to another of the same species, variations do occur. In the normal *Pomacanthus imperator* juvenile there are complete white circles or ovals. However, at times the apparatus that controls color pattern development goes slightly astray and produces a different pattern, although the fish so affected are still recognizable as emperor angelfishes. Similarly, color variants of the blue Koran angelfish, *Pomacanthus semicirculatus,* differ from the more usual pattern. *Genicanthus lamarck* has several variations, depending upon the width of the black lines on the body or the presence or absence of the black edging to the upper and lower edges of the tail fin. The two individuals seen in figure 24 show some of these differences.

Spawning behavior of the angelfishes has never been reported. Even though many hours of underwater observation on the coral reefs have been spent, actual spawning sequences have not been ob-

10. *Pomacanthus imperator* (Bloch). 180 mm standard length. Ogasawara Islands. The final adult color pattern is now evident along with an extension of the dorsal fin into a point, another adult characteristic.

11. *Pomacanthus semicirculatus* (Cuvier & Valenciennes). 35 mm standard length. Okinawa. The typical juvenile form of the Koran angelfish.

14

served (or recognized). It is known that the eggs are free-floating and that the larvae develop offshore in deeper waters. At a certain time the larvae reach an age at which they are ready to metamorphose, and they then appear inshore as tiny juvenile angelfishes with recognizable color patterns. This offshore development aids the species in their distribution. Ocean currents carry off some of the larvae to places which they would not be able to reach as adults. In the summer months reef fishes can be found farther north than in the winter, when the cold water prohibits their spread.

Because of their timidity and the closeness of the coral formations into which they can escape, angelfishes are usually difficult to capture. Individuals of the genus *Centropyge* can be seen around coral reefs quite frequently, but they disappear quickly upon a diver's approach. They seem to know their territory quite well and are able to escape capture by swimming into their 'holes' only to reappear a short distance away from one of their alternate exits.

The larger angelfishes usually have long, filamentous (or at least pointed) fins. Their bodies are compressed (flattened laterally), and the mouth is small. Besides the large, strong spine on the corner of the preopercular bone, other head bones are provided with short, but sharp, spines. It is not known whether any of these spines are useful to the fish for protection. A deep-bodied fish like an angelfish is a difficult fish to swallow, especially if it faces its enemy with dorsal spines erected . . . and this is exactly what they do. When danger threatens and they cannot escape, angelfishes confront the attacker with the head down and the erected dorsal fin spines facing the enemy.

Even with such conspicuous forms and color patterns, new angelfishes are still being found today. Figures 19-22, for example, are three angelfishes that have been described in recent years by Japanese ichthyologists. Another new species is being presented here for the first time by Randall & Burgess.

12. *Pomacanthus semicirculatus* (Cuvier & Valenciennes). 20 mm standard length.

13. *Pomacanthus semicirculatus* (Cuvier & Valenciennes). 35 mm standard length.

14. *Pomacanthus semicirculatus* (Cuvier & Valenciennes). 120 mm standard length.

15. *Pomacanthus semicirculatus* (Cuvier Valenciennes). 180 mm standard length.

16. *Euxiphipops sexstriatus* (Cuvier). 40 mm standard length. Okinawa. This and the following two photographs show the change in color pattern of the six-striped angelfish from juvenile to adult.

17. *Euxiphipops sexstriatus* (Cuvier). 70 mm standard length. The combination of juvenile and adult color patterns can clearly be seen in this photograph. This angelfish was photographed 18 months after its first photo above.

18. *Euxiphipops sexstriatus* (Cuvier). 130 mm standard length. Okinawa. The same specimen as the above two photographs but two years after it was collected. The juvenile color pattern is completely lost.

19. *Genicanthus fucosus* (Yasuda & Tominaga). 129 mm standard length. The Japanese Swallow is a recently discovered angelfish. This is an adult fish, the Juveniles still being unknown. It was first discovered at Miyake Island.

20. *Holacanthus venustus* Yasuda & Tominaga. 77 mm standard length. This blue-and-yellow angelfish is another new angelfish. The fish shown here apparently is not an adult although no color changes are expected in this species with further growth. It was discovered at Izu-Oshima Island and later also found at Ishigaki Island.

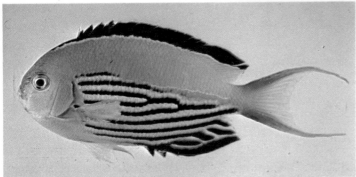

21. *Genicanthus watanabei* (Yasuda & Tominaga). 100 mm standard length. Okinawa. The adult male of the black-edge angelfish is quite distinct.

22. *Genicanthus watanabei* (Yasuda & Tominaga). 90 mm standard length. Okinawa. The adult female is less ornate than the male black-edge angelfish.

23. *Centropyge heraldi* Woods & Schultz. 40 mm standard length. Okinawa. Herald's angelfish is often mistaken for the Lemonpeel, *Centropyge flavissimus*, but it lacks the blue ring around the eyes and the blue edging to the fins.

24. *Genicanthus lamark* (Lacépède). 150 mm standard length. Okinawa. Lamark's angelfish is rare and not usually encountered on the reef. This species has also been reported from Kochi.

25. *Genicanthus lamark* (Lacépède). About 150 mm standard length. Ishigaki Island. Two Lamark's angelfishes in their natural habitat. Whether these two fishes represent a male-female pair is not known.

26. *Centropyge heraldi* Woods & Schultz. 40 mm standard length. Okinawa. The cheek, spines very evident in this photograph, may be used in defensive maneuvers. It is also the characteristics which immediately distinguishes the angelfishes from the butterflyfishes.

27. *Genicanthus semifasciatus* Kamohara. 120 mm standard length. This half-striped angelfish was reported from Kochi. It is not common.

28. *Centropyge flavissimus*
(Cuvier & Valenciennes).
40mm standard length.
Pescadores, Taiwan. This is
the true lemonpeel angelfish
one of the most attractive
of the smaller angelfish
species. Young males have
a black spot on their sides.

29. *Centropyge vroliki*
(Bleeker). 40 mm standard
length. Okinawa. The
pearl-scaled angelfish is very
common in Pacific waters.
It may have cross-bred
with the lemonpeel
producing hybrids that are
yellow with a dark posterior.

30. *Centropyge ferrugatus*
Randall & Burgess, new
species. 30 mm standard
length. Okinawa. This
beautiful species is also
known from Amami-Oshima
Island. Its common name is
the rusty angelfish, and
was discovered as a new
species by Dr. John Randall.

Centropyge ferrugatus Randall & Burgess, new species.

Holotype. — BPBM 6831, adult, 70.5 mmSL, Ishigaki, Ryukyu Islands. Collected by Dr. John E. Randall, May 25, 1968, on a reef about ½ mile off the harbor of Ishigaki City, 30-60 feet deep, using quinaldine.

Paratype. — BPBM 6831, adult, 58.3 mm SL, Ishigaki, Ryukyu Islands. Same data as holotype.

Description. — Dorsal fin rays XIV, 17; anal fin rays III, 17-18; pectoral fin rays 16; 43-45 scales in longitudinal series from upper edge of operculum to base of caudal fin; 20-23 gill rakers.

Depth 1.8-1.9, head 3.8, caudal peduncle depth 7.0-7-3, all in standard length; eye 2.4-3.1, snout 2.8-3.0, interorbital width 2.5-2.8, all in head length.

Lacrimal with several (3-6) short but strong spines on lower and posterior edges; interopercle with small spines (3) at anterior end; preopercle with one or two large and one small spine on lower edge, upper arm lined with small spines; dorsal and anal fins angular as adult, the posterior edges vertical; caudal truncate; lateral line complete or with separate section on caudal peduncle.

Color Pattern. — As seen in figures 30 and 31. Color of living animals also shown.

Remarks. — This species differs from all other species of *Centropyge* by color pattern. By virtue of its fin shape it appears to belong to a group of deep-water species of the genus *Centropyge*, recently collected in relatively deep water by Dr. Randall, as yet undescribed.

Photograph (fig. 31) is of the holotype.

(ferrugat — iron-red).

31. *Centropyge ferrugatus* Randall & Burgess. 73 mm standard length. Ryukyu Islands. This new discovery may have a wider distribution than currently known. Its habitat is the coral reef. Photo of the type by Dr. John E. Randall.

32. *Centropyge loriculus* (Günther). About 40 mm standard length. Johnston Atoll. The flaming angelfish is very conspicuous against the blue and green background of the reef. Although this fish is now known from other areas of the Pacific it was first discovered at Johnston Atoll where this photograph was taken. Photo by Warren E. Burgess.

33. *Centropyge loriculus* (Günther). 57 mm standard length. Oahu, Hawaiian Islands. The flaming angelfish was incorrectly described a second time under the name *Centropyge flammeus,* perhaps more descriptive than *loriculus* which takes precedence. Photo by Dr. John E. Randall.

34. *Pygoplites diacanthus* (Boddaert). 200 mm standard length. Pacific Ocean. The strong preopercular spine in this regal angelfish is well contrasted by the blue color against the orange background. Photo by Hans and Klaus Paysan.

35. *Pygoplites diacanthus* (Boddaert). 180 mm standard length. Okinawa. The juveniles of this species are very similar to the adults in color pattern. The only major difference appears to be a dark spot in the dorsal fin which disappears with age.

36. *Centropyge tibicen* (Cuvier & Valenciennes). 40 mm standard length. Okinawa. The keyhole angelfish has also been reported from mainland Japan at Wakayama. The white spot on its side may assume different shapes and may, at times, be completely absent.

37. *Centropyge bicolor* (Bloch). 40 mm standard length. Okinawa. This oriole angelfish is very hard to maintain in captivity.

38. *Pomacanthus annularis* (Bloch). 120 mm standard length. Taiwan. The blue-ringed angelfish undergoes a complete color transformation from juvenile to adult. This photo depicts the adult color pattern.

39. *Holacanthus trimaculatus* (Lacépède). 140 mm standard length. Okinawa. The three-spotted angelfish gets its common name from the two lateral spots, and the third on the forehead.

40. *Centropyge bispinosus* (Günther). 40 mm standard length. Okinawa. This coral beauty extends as far north in Japan as Amami-Oshima Island.

42. *Euxiphipops navarchus* (Cuvier & Valenciennes). 50 mm
standard length. Philippine Islands. This young blue-girdled
angelfish has recently changed from its juvenile color pattern,
remnants of which can still be seen.

41. *Euxiphipops navarchus* (Cuvier & Valenciennes). 130 mm
standard length. Philippine Islands. The magnificently colored
blue-girdled angelfish retains this color pattern for most of
its life. Only the smallest individuals are differently patterned.

43. *Euxiphipops xanthometapon* (Bleeker). 150 mm standard length. Okinawa. The blue-faced angelfish has also been collected at Ishigaki Island, Japan.

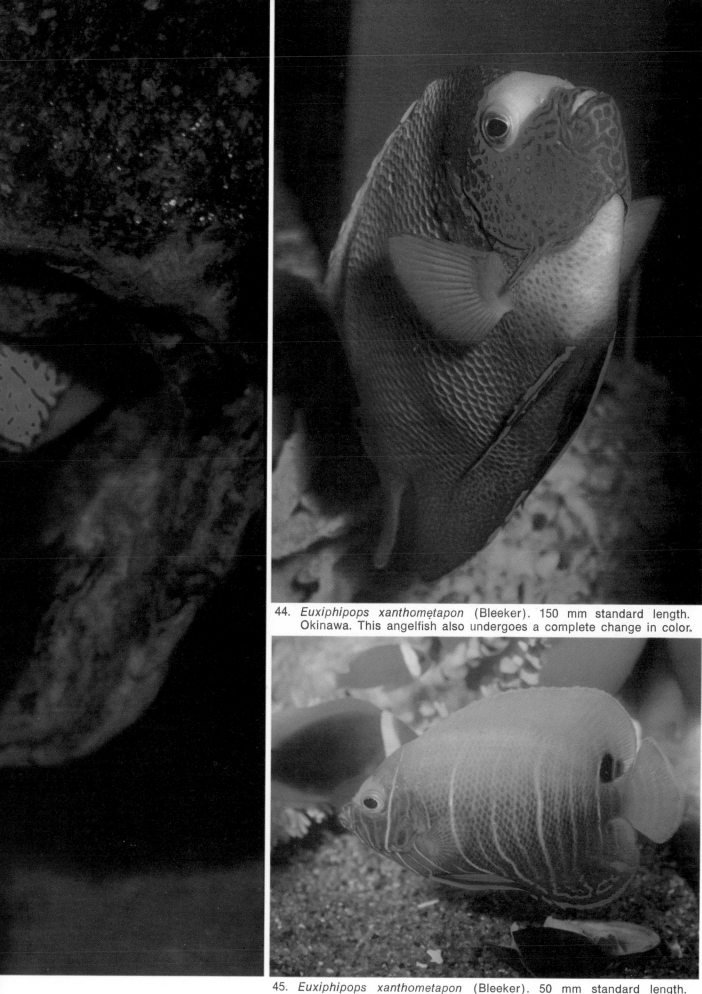

44. *Euxiphipops xanthometapon* (Bleeker). 150 mm standard length. Okinawa. This angelfish also undergoes a complete change in color.

45. *Euxiphipops xanthometapon* (Bleeker). 50 mm standard length. Okinawa. A blue-faced angelfish with both adult and juvenile coloration superimposed.

46. *Chaetodontpolus septentrionalis* (Temminck & Schlegel). 20 mm standard length. Kanagawa. This young blue-striped angelfish bears little resemblance to its adult in the back.

47. *Chaetodontpolus septentrionalis* (Temminck & Schlegel). This young blue-striped angelfish shows the color changes that this species undergoes with age.

48 and 49. *Chaetodontoplus septentrionalis* (Temminck & Schlegel). Further stages in the development of this species. After 6 months in captivity this angelfish has now lost most of its juvenile plumage.

50 and 51. *Chaetodontoplus septentrionalis* (Temminck & Schlegel). The adult color pattern of the blue-lined angelfish. After about eight months in captivity this individual blue-lined angelfish has completed its color change.

52. *Chaetodontoplus chrysocephalus*
(Bleeker). Izu Marine Park.
The yellow head angelfish is often
confused with the blue-lined
angelfish particularly due to the
blue lines present on the head.
Some scientists speculate that this
may be a hybrid between
C. septentrionalis and *melanosoma.*

53. *Chaetodontoplus melanosoma*
(Bleeker). 25 mm standard length.
Izu Marine Park. Many angelfishes
change color with age and this
one is no exception. This and the
following photograph show the
juvenile and adult color patterns
of the brown angelfish.

54. *Chaetodontoplus melanosoma*
(Bleeker). 130 mm standard
length. Philippines. The adult
brown angelfish. It has lost the
yellow bar across the pectoral
fin base that is seen in the
juvenile above and there is less
of a yellow border to the dorsal,
anal, and caudal fins.

55. *Chaetodontoplus mesoleucus* (Bloch). 40 mm standard length. Okinawa. The vermiculated angelfish is also known as far north in Japan as the Amami-Oshima Island. Although closely related to other species of the genus *Chaetodontoplus* this fish apparently does not undergo the color metamorphosis of those species.

56. *Chaetodontoplus mesoleucus* (Bloch). 50mm standard length. Okinawa. The vermiculated angelfish is common in its range from Singapore to the Philippine Islands. Notice how the wide black band completely cbscures the eye. This may aid in protecting this vital organ from the attacks of enemies.

57. *Centropyge flavicauda* Fraser-Brunner. Ito.
This rather rare species appears to be closely
related to *Centropyge potteri* of the Hawaiian
Islands. There are several instances where
the Japanese fauna appears to be close to
the Hawaiian fauna.

58. *Chaetodontoplus mesoleucus* (Bloch). About
90 mm standard length. Indo-Pacific. The
red-tailed variety of the vermiculated angelfish is less common than the yellow-tailed
form. It may be a geographical subspecies
or the result of a different diet. Photo by the
Malaya Straits Times in the Raffles Aquarium
in Singapore.

Forehead-pushing, one of the types of aggressive behavior patterns distinguished in various species of chaetodontids studied, was exhibited only by *Heniochus acuminatus* (shown here) and *Chelmon rostatus*. Photo by Tierfreunde.

Family CHAETODONTIDAE
BUTTERFLYFISHES

Butterflyfishes are small fishes of the coral reef, the largest rarely exceeding one foot in length. They undergo some color changes with growth, but not to such an extent as in the angelfishes.

Butterflyfishes are usually deep bodied fishes with small mouths set with slender needle-like teeth. These teeth are in several rows in each jaw, like those of the angelfishes, also giving the appearance of a brush. This characteristic is the one which provides the name chaetodonts (*chaeta*= bristle; *odont*=tooth), or bristle-tooth. Their food is small invertebrates which they nibble or pick from the reefs. Among the major invertebrate food items are coral polyps. A lack of coral polyps in the food supplied to some captive butterflyfishes leads to their decline and eventual death. Some of the butterflyfishes, the long-nosed and beaked species, have special adaptations in their elongated snouts whereby they can reach into coral crevices and holes to obtain small animals that most other species cannot reach.

Color changes are not as dramatic in butterflyfishes as in angelfishes. They may lose a spot or stripe with growth but usually are recognizable while they are still juveniles. A theory has arisen concerning the black spot in the fin or on the posterior end of the body. The spot is supposed to represent a false eye, the true eye being hidden in a black stripe crossing the head. An attacker is supposedly decoyed by this spot, thinking it is a real eye. The strike is thus directed at the wrong end of the body, the butterflyfish making good its escape during the confusion.

The larval butterflyfishes have bony plates covering their heads, giving them a peculiar appearance quite different from that of the juveniles or adults. This larval form was described as a new genus of fishes, *Tholichthys,* and the name is still retained as a common term for this stage.

Although seemingly devoid of any means of protection against enemies, butterflyfishes are able to survive the rigorous life of the reef. They are quick and agile, easily disappearing into the coral and rock formations that are always close by. Their deep, narrow bodies fit into narrow openings in the reef, much as do those of the angelfishes. When cornered, they lower the head and spread their spines, presenting the attacker with the sharp points. A butterflyfish with the first few spines missing is occasionally seen on the reef; the missing spines probably were lost to some enemy.

Juvenile butterflyfishes are known as part-time parasite pickers. Like the true cleaner wrasse, *Labroides,* they remove parasites from other, larger fishes. But the butterflyfishes practice this only occasionally, not full time like the wrasses.

In the butterflyfish genus *Heniochus* the fourth dorsal fin spine develops into an elongate filament. This filament is quite long in *Heniochus acuminatus,* being longer than the body itself. In addition, this genus has species in which bony protuberances or horns develop with age.

Many species of butterflyfishes form pairs. The two fishes of a pair stay together around an area of reef which might be considered a territory. If one stops to feed and the other swims on, the first one will usually hurry to catch up to the other, almost as if they were attached with a rubber band.

59. *Chaetodon aureus*. Temminck & Schlegel   70 mm standard length. Okinawa. Butterflyfishes, such as this species, undergo some changes with age. This and the next two photographs are of the same species, although different ages. The adult is shown here.

60. *Chaetodon aureus* Temminck & Schlegel. 15 mm standard length. Kanagawa. This very young golden butterflyfish looks quite different than the adult pictured above, or the semi-adult in the photo to the right. All butterflyfishes have what is known as a *tholichthys* larva in which the head is armored with bony plates.

61. *Chaetodon aureus* Temminck & Schlegel. 30 mm standard length. Kanagawa. The large black spot in the dorsal fin of this juvenile golden butterflyfish will disappear as the fish grows older, as can be seen in Figure 59.

62. *Chaetodon speculum* Cuvier & Valenciennes. 40 mm standard length. Okinawa. There are several butterfly-fishes with a large black spot on their sides. This one, the oval-spot butterflyfish, is from the western Pacific Ocean. The body is almost entirely yellow. This species has been collected as far north as Kaminato in Chiba, Japan.

63. *Chaetodon kleinii* Bloch. 30 mm standard length. Shizuoka. Klein's butterflyfish is widespread in the tropical parts of the Indian and Pacific Oceans and is fairly common throughout its range. There is no color change with age in this species.

64. *Hemitaurichthys polylepis* (Bleeker). 60 mm standard length. Okinawa. This species of butterflyfish changes its head color from yellow to dark brown. In this photograph it is in an intermediate stage.

65. *Chaetodon melanotus* Bloch & Schneider. 30 mm standard length. Kanagawa. The black-backed butterflyfish when frightened will become very dark in the upper parts of its body except for two pale spots. The individual in this photograph is doing well in captivity and shows its best coloration.

66. *Chaetodon lineolatus* Cuvier & Valenciennes. 30 mm standard length. Okinawa. This young lined-butterflyfish will change only slightly with age. The adult is shown in the photograph to the right for comparison. The lined butterflyfish is the largest of the butterflyfishes reaching a size of over a foot in length.

67. *Chaetodon lineolatus* Cuvier & Valenciennes. 120 mm standard length. Okinawa. This species extends as far north as Misaki, Kanagawa, Japan. Lined butterflyfishes are usually found in pairs.

68. *Chaetodon unimaculatus* Bloch. 70 mm standard length. Okinawa. The teardrop butterflyfish has the large black spot on its side similar to that of *Chaetodon speculum*. It differs from that species in having the lower part of the body white and an extension of the spot ventrally forming the teardrop of the common name.

69. *Chaetodon reticulatus* Cuvier & Valenciennes. 30 mm standard length. Ogasawara Islands. The reticulated butterflyfish has a bright red-orange spot at the base of the anal fin (only slightly indicated in this photograph). This juvenile will not change color very much with age.

70. *Chaetodon ephippium* Cuvier &
Valenciennes. 40 mm standard
length. Okinawa. The saddle
butterflyfish is one of the most
colorful of butterflyfishes. It is
found only in the Pacific Ocean,
being replaced in the Indian
Ocean by a close relative,
C. xanthocephalus. The eye band
disappears with age.

71. *Chaetodon ephippium* Cuvier &
Valenciennes. 15 mm standard
length. Okinawa. This very young
saddle butterflyfish probably has
just transformed from its
tholichthys stage. The changes
with age are indicated in figures
70 and 77.

72. *Chaetodon trifascialis* Quoy & Gaimard. 108 mm standard length. Tahiti. The adult chevron butterflyfish has a pointed dorsal fin and lacks the black posterior band of the juvenile (fig. 111). This species is one of the two butterflyfishes that have four anal spines instead of the more normal number of three. Photo by Dr. John E. Randall.

73. *Chaetodon mertensii* Cuvier. 91 mm standard length. Eniwetok, Marshall Islands. The chevron pattern occurs in several species of butterflyfishes. This may indicate a close relationship or at least a common ancestor. Photo by Dr. John E. Randall.

74. *Chaetodon ephippium* Cuvier & Valenciennes. Adult. The saddle butterflyfish usually occurs in pairs such as these two photographed at Johnston Atoll in the central Pacific Ocean. The filament in these individuals is fully grown. Photo by Warren E. Burgess.

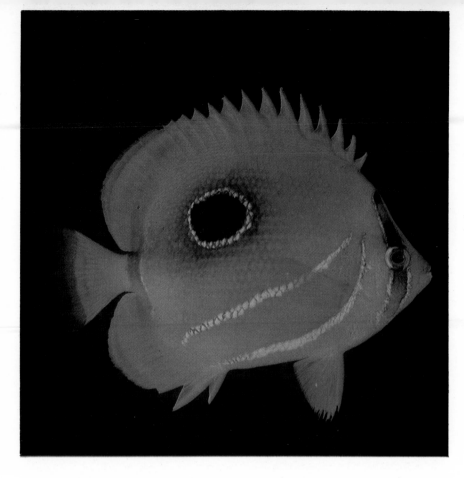

75. *Chaetodon bennetti* Cuvier and Valenciennes. 112 mm standard length. Tahiti. Bennett's butterflyfish is not common anywhere although it has a very wide distribution throughout the tropical areas of the Pacific and Indian Ocean. Photo by Dr. John E. Randall.

76. *Chaetodon multicinctus* Garrett. 74 mm standard length. Hawaiian Islands. This Hawaiian butterflyfish bears a striking resemblance to *Chaetodon punctatofasciatus* (fig. 83) and is no doubt related to that species. Photo by Dr. John E. Randall.

77. *Chaetodon ephippium* Cuvier & Valenciennes. 130 mm standard length. Okinawa. As the saddle butterflyfish grows it develops a filamentous extension of the dorsal fin. This individual has a short spike in the fin which is either just starting to grow or has been bitten off by a tank-mate. Notice that the eyeband has almost disappeared. The lower fish in the photo is *Chaetodon nippon*.

78. *Chaetodon quadrimaculatus* Gray. 130 mm standard length. Ogasawara Islands. The four-spot butterflyfish is not very common and found in the central and western Pacific Ocean. The two white spots on each side of the body give this fish its common name.

79. *Chaetodon lunula* (Lacépède). 20 mm standard length. Kominato, Chiba, Japan. The raccoon butterflyfish undergoes some changes with age. Compare this juvenile with the photograph on the opposite page of the adult (fig. 80).

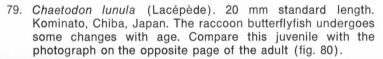

80. *Chaetodon lunula* (Lacépède). 150 mm standard length. Okinawa. The adult raccoon butterflyfish is easily recognizable. Notice the absence of the dorsal fin spot of the juvenile.

81. *Chaetodon rafflesi* Bennett. 80 mm standard length. Okinawa. Raffles butterflyfish has a distinctly reticulated pattern, each scale being outlined with a darker color than the general body color.

82. *Chaetodon falcula* Bloch 40 mm standard length. Okinawa. The double-saddle butterflyfish is common in the tropical Pacific Ocean. It almost always is found as pairs.

83. *C h a e t o d o n punctatofasciatus* Cuvier & Valenciennes. 40 mm standard length. Okinawa. This spot-banded butterflyfish is one of the smaller species of butterfly-fishes reaching only about five to six inches in length.

84. *Chaetodon daedalma* Jordan & Fowler. 40 mm standard length. Ogasawara Islands. The wrought-iron butterflyfish is known only from Japan. Its distinctive color pattern makes one think of a pre-historic animal of some kind.

85. *Chaetodon auriga* Forskål. 100 mm standard length. Okinawa. The filament butterflyfish is common and wide-ranging. In Japan the northernmost extension of this species is to Wakayama. The adult filament butterflyfish has an extension of some dorsal fin rays into a filament.

86. *Chaetodon trifasciatus* Park. 35 mm standard length. Okinawa. It is a delicate fish and does poorly in aquaria where live coral cannot be offered.

87. *Chaetodon auriga* Forskål. 30 mm standard length. Misaki, Kanegawa. The younger stages of the filament butterflyfish lacks the filament of the adult, otherwise it closely resembles the older fishes.

88. *Chaetodon vagabundus* Linnaeus. 20 mm standard length. Misaki, Kanagawa, Japan.

89. *Chaetodon vagabundus* Linnaeus. 80 mm standard length. Okinawa. The vagabond butterflyfish is found in the tropical areas of the Pacific and Indian Ocean. It is a hardy fish and lives well in aquaria.

90. *Chaetodon adiergastos* Seale. 120 mm standard length. Okinawa. The Philippine butterflyfish is distinctive in having the black horseshoe-shaped marking on its nape. The juvenile (next photograph) is different in some aspects of the color pattern. The range of this butterflyfish is not large, being only from the East Indies and Philippine Islands to southern Japan.

91. *Chaetodon adiergastos* Seale. 30 mm standard length. Okinawa. This juvenile Philippine butterflyfish has a dark spot in its dorsal fin and lacks the black marking on the nape of the adult. The common name of course refers to the locality where it was first discovered and not the entire range.

92. *Chaetodon triangulum* Cuvier & Valenciennes. 50 mm standard length. Okinawa. The triangle butterflyfish is very attractive but unfortunately does not do well in captivity. It is very deep bodied but thin, a useful shape when slipping into a narrow crevice to escape an enemy.

93. *Chaetodon triangulum* Cuvier & Valenciennes. 25 mm standard length. There is very little difference between this very young individual and the fish in the previous photograph, (fig. 92) nearly twice its size. The adult color pattern is exactly the same as that fish.

94. *Chaetodon ornatissimus* Cuvier & Valenciennes. Adult. Johnston Atoll. The ornate butterflyfishes eat coral polyps as one of this pair is doing. The permanent pair is formed at least by the time the fish reaches a length of 3–4 inches. Photo by Warren E. Burgess.

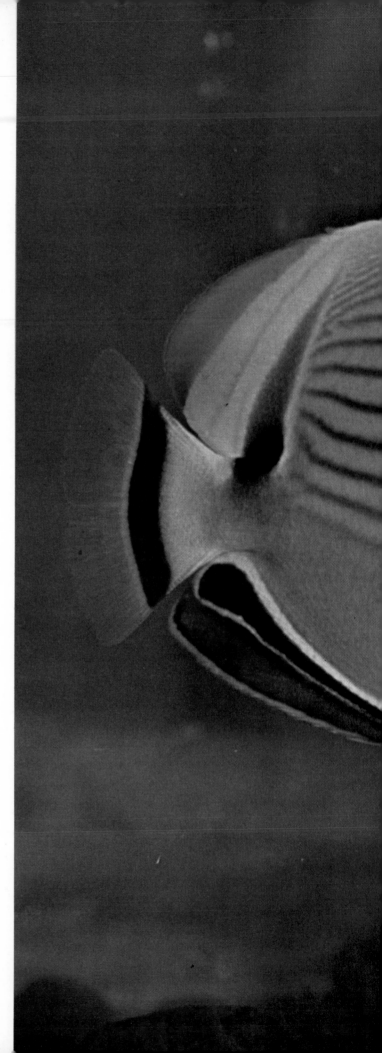

95. *Chaetodon trifasciatus* Park. Adult. Indo-Pacific region. The three-striped butterflyfish is very difficult to maintain in captivity. The banding of the head region is similar to that of the ornate butterflyfish (fig. 94). Photo by Dr. Herbert R. Axelrod.

96. *Chaetodon modestus*
Temminck & Schlegel.
50 mm standard
length. This
butterflyfish is found
in Japan and
southward to the
Philippines and
Singapore. This one
was photographed at
the Izu Marine Park,
Japan.

97. *Coradion fulvocinctus*
Tanaka. 30 mm
standard length. Izu
Marine Park. This
species should not be
confused with the
ocellate butterflyfish
*Parachaetodon
ocellatus*. They both
have similar shapes
but the color pattern is
different (see fig. 104).

98. *Chaetodon xanthurus* Bleeker. 40 mm standard length. Okinawa. The crosshatch butterflyfish is more common in the Philippine Islands than any other area of its range. It can easily be distinguished from the following species on color pattern alone although the two are still often confused.

99. *Chaetodon mertensii* Cuvier. 40 mm standard length. Ishigaki Island. Although Merten's butterflyfish is more common in the Pacific Islands it becomes rarer as the Asian continent is neared. It is closely related to the crosshatch butterflyfish above.

100. *Chaetodon semeion* Bleeker. 40 mm standard length. Okinawa. The dotted butterflyfishes is one of the rarer butterflyfishes of the Pacific. In larger individuals there is a slender filament extending from the middle edge of the dorsal fin.

101. *Chaetodon bennetti* Cuvier & Valenciennes. 30 mm standard length. Okinawa. Bennett's butterflyfish is another tropical Pacific butterflyfish. Although other butterflyfishes may have a black lateral spot this species has a pair of bright blue lines on its side meeting in a "V". The juvenile is similar to the adult.

102. *Chaetodon ornatissimus* Cuvier & Valenciennes. 70 mm standard length. Okinawa. The ornate butterflyfish is well deserving of its name with bright orange stripes against a pure white background. It is short snouted for a butterflyfish and must rely on surface animals for food. Coral polyps form a large part of its diet.

103. *Chaetodon plebeius* Cuvier & Valenciennes. 40 mm standard length. Okinawa. The lateral spot on this species of butterflyfish is more diffuse and a second spot is present on the caudal peduncle.

104. *Parachaetodon ocellatus* (Cuvier). 30 mm standard length. Philippine Islands. It is distinct among the butter-flyfishes in having only six dorsal fin spines, all others having at least nine and as many as sixteen.

105. *Chaetodon argentatus* Smith & Radcliffe. 40 mm standard length. Okinawa.

106. *Chaetodon meyeri* Bloch & Schneider. 70 mm standard length. Ishigaki Island.

107. *Chaetodon guntheri* Ahl. 40 mm standard length. Izu Marine Park.

108. *Chaetodon meyeri* Bloch & Schneider. Juvenile of fig. 106. Photo by Earl Kennedy.

109. *Chaetodon octofasciatus* Bloch. Eight-banded butterflyfish. 30 mm standard length. Okinawa.

110. *Chaetodon nippon* Steindachner & Döderlein. 25 mm standard length. Shizuoka, Japan. The Japanese butter-flyfish is restricted in range from southern Japan to the Philippine Islands. The adult looks very much like this juvenile.

111. *Chaetodon trifascialis* Quoy & Gaimard. 50 mm standard length. Okinawa. Previously known as *Chaetodon strigangulus*.

112. *Chaetodon wiebeli* Kaup. 30 mm. Okinawa. This species is common in the Philippines to Japan area. The juveniles have a dark spot in the dorsal fin.

113. *Forcipiger flavissimus* Jordan & McGregor. 120 mm standard length. Okinawa. The long-nosed butterflyfish
has a long snout which it may use to obtain small invertebrates from holes or crevices unreachable by fishes
with a normal sized snout.

114. *Heniochus acuminatus* (Linnaeus). 120 mm standard length. Aburatsubo Marine Park, Japan. This pennant butterflyfish is an abberant individual. Normally only the fourth dorsal fin spine is elongated into a filament. In this specimen there appears to be two spines elongated.

115. *Heniochus varius* (Cuvier). 40 mm standard length. Okinawa. The sea-bull receives its common name from the prominent protuberance at the nape and the strong horns that develop above the eyes. In this juvenile these characters have not developed fully as yet.

116. *Heniochus chrysostomus* Cuvier & Valenciennes. 30 mm standard length. Okinawa. This butterflyfish has previously been known as *Heniochus permutatus.*

117. *Heniochus singularius* Smith & Radcliffe. 30 mm standard length. Okinawa. The singular butterflyfish apparently is restricted in its range to southeast Asia from Japan to the East Indies.

118. *Heniochus monoceros* Cuvier & Valenciennes. 30 mm standard length. Okinawa. The juvenile masked butterflyfish closely resembles the adult (see fig. 120). Larger individuals of this species develop the characteristic horns of the genus as well as the protuberance on the nape.

119. *Heniochus monoceros* Cuvier & Valenciennes. 30 mm standard length. Okinawa. A frontal view of the same individual showing the distinctive pattern of dark brown and white. The masked butterflyfish can be found on coral reefs usually hiding in holes or caves beneath the corals.

120. *Heniochus monoceros* Cuvier & Valenciennes. 150 mm standard length. Aburatsubo Marine Park, Japan. The marking on the face of this masked butterflyfish make it easily distinguishable from the other species in this genus. This is an adult.

121. *Chaetodon citrinellus* Cuvier & Valenciennes. 30 mm standard length. Okinawa. The citron butterflyfish is easily recognized by the wide black band along the edge of the anal fin.

122. *Chelmon rostratus* (Linnaeus). 70 mm standard length. Philippine Islands. The beaked butterflyfish is similarly endowed as the long-snouted butterflyfish for the acquisition of food.

Family SCORPIDIDAE
SWEEPS

Most of the fishes in this family are found only in Australia. They are small fishes with small mouths provided with rows of slender teeth, the outer row enlarged. The main diet of the sweeps consists of small invertebrate animals.

The species represented here, *Microcanthus strigatus,* better known as the stripey, was once thought to be a member of the butterflyfish family. In 1945, however, a scientist by the name of Fraser-Brunner proved this fish to be a scorpidid.

The stripey is found in southern Japan and Hawaii, a distribution that has caused scientists to believe that the Hawaiian fishes came, in part, from the warmer areas of Japan via a warm water current like the Kuroshio current now in existence.

In Hawaii the stripey is a shore form that appears in tidal pools early in the spring. There are no remarkable color changes with age and no specialized larval form. It is a hardy species, well suited to aquarium life. The stripey grows rapidly and can withstand adverse aquarium conditions. When first appearing in the tide pools, stripeys are about half an inch in length, their color pattern relatively complete. In four months, it is said, they can grow to a length of two inches.

Although the stripey is strictly a shore form, commonly occurring around rocky and coral areas, other members of the family inhabit more open waters.

Family MONODACTYLIDAE
MOONFISHES

The moonfishes are small, silvery fishes with deep bodies and small mouths. The dorsal and anal fins are opposite and equal, the first rays produced slightly. The pelvic fins are reduced or rudimentary.

The moonfishes inhabit shore waters and can easily adapt to pure fresh-water, wandering up rivers beyond the influence of salt water.

The most common species of moonfish is *Monodactylus argenteus.* It is a common aquarium favorite, doing quite well in fresh, salt, or brackish water. It reaches a length of about seven inches. When several individuals are kept together they form a small school. In nature, schools of moonfishes can be seen around docks and ships at anchor, and frequently around the roots of mangrove trees.

Moonfishes have been spawned in aquaria and the young raised to maturity. The eggs are small and spherical and float when released. The young are tiny replicas of the adults, and development proceeds directly.

When frightened, the moonfish can undergo some color changes. The silver color is replaced by a slaty-gray or blackish color. This is very frustrating to a photographer attempting to take their picture. The photographer must wait until the fish quiets down and returns to its original colors. In addition, the black bars, particularly the one through the pectoral fin base, may fade out and completely disappear.

Monodactylus sebae, from the west coast of Africa (not represented by a photograph), is deeper-bodied than *M. argenteus* and has an extra black bar towards the posterior end of the body. It has similar habits of staying around docks of harbors and entering rivers.

Family ZANCLIDAE
MOORISH IDOLS

The Moorish idol, *Zanclus canescens,* is the only species included in this family. It is a very beautiful fish, highly prized by aquarists, but usually very difficult to maintain in captivity.

The beauty of this fish has prompted artists and designers to use it in their artistic endeavors, surpassed in representation only by the sea horse.

The long, filamentous extension of one of the dorsal spines is reminiscent of the butterflyfish species *Heniochus acuminatus.* This does not mean they are closely related, however, being just an example of similar structures in different fishes.

The snout of the Moorish idol is drawn out to some extent, and, like the butterflyfishes, *Zanclus* can eat small invertebrates that other short-snouted fishes cannot reach. Besides the invertebrates, the diet of the Moorish idol includes a large proportion of vegetable matter, principally filamentous algae. The teeth are slender and set in brush-like rows.

The Moorish idol, again like the species of *Heniochus,* has short horns above the eyes.

Moorish idols are commonly encountered around the coral reef in small groups of three to ten or more. They browse along the reef, nibbling here and there on the coral rocks, moving off to better feeding grounds when they have picked a certain section clean of their most desirable food items. When frightened they dart off quickly, moving about the coral formations with extraordinary agility; this makes persuit very difficult, if not impossible.

At night, Moorish idols rest on the bottom, apparently asleep. Their color appears darker, and they may be resting with the head under part of the coral. At this time it is relatively easy to approach them. One of the authors (WEB) was able to pick up an individual by hand at night, although when it awakened it was able to free itself and swim away.

The young Moorish idol is a part-transparent part-silvery larva, spending much of its early life in the open ocean waters. It returns to the reef at a certain age to metamorphose into a recognizable juvenile. These larvae are referred to as the "acronurus" stage of the Moorish idol and also of surgeonfishes, family Acanthuridae. The Moorish idol acronurus has the long, filamentous ray of the dorsal fin. It is quite large, 40-50 mm in length, when ready to metamorphose. This is the reason that very small Moorish idols are never seen.

123. *Microcanthus strigatus* (Cuvier & Valenciennes). About 30–40 mm standard length. Aburatsubo, Kanagawa. The stripey was once considered a butterflyfish but since 1945 has been a member of the family Scorpididae. Although absent from all other central Pacific Islands this species is common in the Hawaiian Islands.

124. *Monodactylus argenteus* (Linnaeus). 40 mm standard length. Ishigaki Island.

125. *Microcanthus strigatus* (Cuvier & Valenciennes). 30 mm standard length. Kanagawa. Although there is more yellow color in this photo of the stripey than the one above the differences are mainly due to the photographic process rather than an inherent difference in the fishes themselves.

126. *Zanclus canescens* (Linnaeus). 30 mm standard length. Okinawa. The Moorish idol is common in the tropical Pacific and Indian Oceans. Its great beauty make it a prized fish in aquaria. Unfortunately it does not do well in captivity unless fed live mussels. The elongated dorsal ray is sometimes longer than the length of the fish itself.

Family PLATACIDAE
BATFISHES

The batfishes are distinguished by their elongate dorsal and anal fins and deep body, which makes their general shape higher than long. Juveniles have extra-long fins, the proportion between depth and length of the fish becoming lesser with age. Batfishes grow to a size of two feet or more and in some areas of southeast Asia are considered as food for human consumption.

Batfishes eat a variety of foods, including garbage or even offal when available. This wide acceptance of a variety of food is helpful to aquarists. In captivity the batfishes do very well and soon grow to a large size. Many people are able to make "pets" of these fishes, getting them to eat morsels of food from their fingers.

Batfishes are excellent mimics. One, *Platax orbicularis,* resembles the dead leaves of mangrove trees that drop into the water. To enhance the effect of the mimicry, *Platax orbicularis* "plays dead" when alarmed, floating on its side among the leaves. Even when looking for these fishes, it is hard to distinguish between them and the leaves, and one must poke at a suspected 'leaf' to see if it will suddenly swim away.

Platax teira, the long-finned batfish, has exceptionally elongate fins, the height of a juvenile being several times its length. The pelvic fins of this species are elongated as well. It can be found in habitats similar to those of *Platax orbicularis,* that is, mangrove areas and harbors (sometimes even if they are polluted).

The orange-ring batfish has the same type of long fins as *Platax teira,* but the color pattern is quite different. Juvenile *Platax pinnatus,* called orange-ring batfish, are a deep velvety black color with an orange trim around the entire edge of the fish. It is a beautiful fish that certainly would stand out in its environment and could not mimic leaves in the same way as its relatives mentioned above. But it does! It not only goes through the same motions as the other species, but there usually is dead and blackened vegetation on the bottom which provides a background in which this fish can virtually disappear.

Besides the three species mentioned, there appears to be only one other batfish, *Platax batavianus.* This species is poorly known and may turn out to be the adult of one of the other batfishes.

Batfishes all seem to have one color characteristic in common. There is a dark band through the eye, and another through the pectoral fin base. This pattern will appear in *Platax pinnatus* as well when that fish becomes faded with age. The bands may appear or disappear with the mood of the fish, or perhaps as a further copying of the color of the dead leaves.

Although all batfishes are normally found around mangrove habitats, one of the authors (WEB) has seen *Platax pinnatus* on the coral reef in the Philippine Islands. It was an adult and remained hidden in a large coral formation, in the shadows. It would not come out into the open. With such a dark color pattern, perhaps this species may come out at night, when it would be very difficult to see.

When keeping batfishes in captivity it is best to give them plenty of room. They grow large fast and soon require plenty of space for swimming. They are timid fishes and should not be kept with aggressive species which would soon make the long flowing fins very ragged.

127. *Platax teira* (Forskål). Subadult. Philippine Islands. As the long-finned batfish grows the fins in proportion to the body size becomes smaller. Like other batfish this species is an excellent mimic of floating leaves or other vegetation. It grows about one inch per month. Photo by Earl Kennedy.

128. *Platax pinnatus* (Linnaeus). 40 mm standard length. Amami-Oshima Island. The long fins of the batfish are characteristic of the family. This orange-ringed batfish is the most beautiful species in the family, the orange color contrasting sharply with the black of the fins and body. The standard length given is misleading since the greatest dimension of this fish is vertical which is about $3\frac{1}{2}$ times the standard length.

129. *Platax pinnatus* (Linnaeus). 115 mm standard length. This larger orange-ringed batfish from Okinawa has lost some of the black color on its body. This paling can continue until the fish is silvery colored with broad dark bands on head and body. The orange periphery remains as the identifying characteristic of this species of batfish.

130. *Platax teira* (Forskål). 50 mm standard length. Philippine Islands. Similar in fin development to the orange-ringed batfish, the long-finned batfish lacks the orange edging to the fins and never turns solid black.

131. *Platax orbicularis* (Forskål). 40 mm standard length. Okinawa. By far the most common of the batfishes is the round batfish. The color pattern is similar to the dead leaves floating on the surface along the shore where this species is found. The behavior of the round batfish of lying on its side motionless makes it look amazingly like those leaves. This mimicry has no doubt saved this fish from many predators.

132. *Platax orbicularis* (Forskål). 40 mm standard length. Amami-Oshima. A similar sized round batfish with the second bar evident crossing the base of the pectoral fin. It still retains the 'dead leaf' color over most of its body.

133. *Platax orbicularis* (Forskål). 160 mm standard length. At times the batfish will change into a purely black and white pattern as in this photograph. Specimens swimming around a reef will usually have this pattern. The round batfish grows quickly and adapts well to captivity.

Family ACANTHURIDAE

SURGEONFISHES

The surgeonfishes are named for the scalpel-like blade, actually a movable spine, at the base of the tail. This spine is directed forward so that a flip of the tail will bring it into play against an enemy. It is said that some of these spines are poisonous to humans and that wounds will lead quickly to infection. The blade appears at an early stage, even young juveniles possessing them. There are no reports of actual sightings of the surgeonfishes using the spine in combat, but it is assumed that that is their purpose. The species in most genera have a single spine, although some have more. *Naso* and *Prionurus* have several on each side, but these are not movable.

The surgeonfishes have a pelagic larval stage called the acronurus, as mentioned in the discussion of the family Zanclidae. These larvae remain in the open waters of the ocean for several weeks before returning to the inshore waters. They arrive partly by means of a current, partly

Zebrasoma desjardinii   G. Marcuse.

by active swimming. Upon reaching the reef, the surgeonfishes change from this silver and transparent stage to the juvenile color pattern in a short time. A second metamorphosis occurs in some species wherein the juvenile color pattern is quite distinct from that of the adults. This occurs in the blue tang of the Caribbean. The juvenile is a bright lemon yellow, the adult bluish.

Some species, such as *Zebrasoma flavescens,* have different color patterns from one geographical area to another. It is bright yellow in some areas, darker in others, and is usually confused with a similar but normally darker-colored species, *Zebrasoma scopas.*

The genus *Naso* has species which undergo very radical changes in form. The adult fishes develop a protuberance on the anterior part of the head, sometimes very elongate. They are aptly called the unicornfishes.

Surgeonfishes are often used for food for human consumption. They do have a

Zebrasoma flavescens.   Dr. Herbert R. Axelrod.

bad reputation, however, for causing a type of food poisoning called ciguatera. It is not known for sure how the poison is developed or obtained by these fishes, but it is suspected that their algal diet has something to do with it. The toxins contained in the algae are stored by the surgeonfishes rather than eliminated.

Like the batfishes, the surgeonfishes include mimics, *Acanthurus pyroferus* being an example. With its fins folded this surgeonfish bears a striking resemblance to the angelfish *Centropyge vroliki.*

Spawning is accomplished in schools. The surgeonfishes gather at twilight, mill around continuously, and every so often a few members of the group will break away from the school and swim up in the water a short distance, where they release their eggs and sperm.

Surgeonfishes are the grazers of the reef, constantly browsing on different species of algae. Schools of surgeonfishes will pass over the reef in a slow, unhurried movement, each fish searching out some small plantlife and cropping it to its base, leaving the almost denuded part of the reef behind. If a section of reef bottom is protected from the herbivores, a luxurient growth of algae will soon appear.

One of the most colorful of surgeonfishes, *Paracanthurus hepatus,* is bright blue with black and yellow markings. It is quite interesting but, unfortunately, if it does not receive the proper diet it will fade noticeably and remain much of the time at the bottom of the aquarium.

A less delicate species, *Acanthurus lineatus,* is also quite attractive but is not very common.

134. *Acanthurus leucosternon* Bennett. Adult. Indo-Pacific region. The powder-blue surgeonfish is not common at any particular spot but it can be found over a wide geographic area. Photo by Dr. D. Terver of the Nancy Aquarium, France.

135. *Acanthurus nigrofuscus* Forskål. 30 mm standard length. Kanagawa, Japan.

136. *Acanthurus olivaceous* Bloch & Schneider. 40 mm standard length. Kanagawa, Japan.

137. *Acanthurus olivaceous* Bloch & Schneider. 130 mm standard length. Aburatsubo Marine Park, Japan. The adult color pattern is quite different from the juvenile shown in the preceding photograph (fig. 136.). The orange mark is distinctive.

138. *Paracanthurus hepatus* (Linnaeus). 40 mm standard length. Okinawa. The blue tang is probably the most brilliantly colored surgeonfish. It is found on coral reefs.

139. *Prionurus microlepidotus* Lacépède. 100 mm standard length. Kanagawa, Japan. The spiny-tailed tang has three to four pairs of anteriorly directed spines along the caudal peduncle and posterior end of the body. In this fish they are accented by color, possibly as a warning to other fishes that this fish has some razor-sharp dangerous weapons.

140. *Zebrasoma scopas* (Cuvier). 50 mm standard length. Okinawa. The yellow phase of the white-spotted tang is often confused with another species, *Zebrasoma flavescens* (not illustrated). The white spotting and lines are missing in that species however.

141. *Zebrasoma scopas* (Cuvier). 50 mm standard length. Okinawa. The dark color variation of the white-spotted tang is less colorful but more easily distinguished from the yellow tang mentioned above. The characteristic dots and lines are still present however.

142. *Naso lituratus* (Bloch & Schneider). 80 mm standard length. Okinawa. This species never develops the projection from the head as do other unicornfish and has therefore been called the 'smoothhead' unicornfish. The upper and lower edges of the tail become greatly extended in the adult giving it a very streamlined appearance.

143. The yellow surgeonfish in the center of this photograph, *Acanthurus pyroferus,* is an excellent mimic of one of the angelfishes, *Centropyge heraldi* (fig. 23). The fish in the upper right is *Zebrasoma veliferum*, a sailfin tang, the one in the lower left is *Gaterin chaetodontoides,* one of the sweetlips.

144. *Naso unicornis* (Forskål). 200mm standard length. Kominata, Chiba, Japan. The unicornfish is well deserving of its name as can be seen from this photograph. Young unicornfishes do not have this projection.

145. *Acanthurus lineatus* (Linnaeus). 40 mm standard length. Okinawa. Even a beautiful fish such as this one carries a dangerous weapon at the base of its tail.

146. *Naso lituratus* (Bloch & Schneider) Juvenile. Hawaiian Islands. This juvenile smooth-head unicornfish loses the white spots with age and eventually assumes the color pattern of the adult in fig. 142. Photo by Dr. Herbert R. Axelrod.

147. *Acanthurus triostegus* (Linnaeus). Kanagawa. The convict tang, so-called because of its striped pattern is quite common. It passes over the reef in schools of about a hundred fish closely cropping the algae.

148. *Zebrasoma veliferum* (Bloch). 150 mm standard length. The adult has a different color pattern than the juvenile.

149. *Acanthurus japonicus* Schmidt. 70 mm standard length. Okinawa. The common name, white-faced surgeonfish, draws attention to the character which separates this species from its close relative, *Acanthurus glaucopareius* (not illustrated).

150. *Zebrasoma veliferum* (Bloch) to the right. 30 mm standard length. Okinawa. The juvenile sailfin tang is common around reefs easily avoiding capture by hiding among the coral branches.

151. *Lo vulpinus* (Schlegel & Müller). Adult. Indo-Pacific Region. The blotchy appearance over the entire body of the foxface is assumed at night or during periods of stress. Photo by G. Marcuse.

Family SIGANIDAE

RABBITFISHES

Closely allied to the surgeonfishes are the rabbitfishes, family Siganidae. They are easily recognized by the increased number of spines in the pelvic and anal fins. Instead of the usual spine and five-rayed pelvic fins of the perch-like fishes, the rabbitfishes have two spines separated by three soft rays. In the anal fin there are seven spines instead of the more common number of three. The spines are provided with deep grooves on the side. These grooves contain venom glands, and if a person's hand is punctured when handling a rabbitfish, a very painful wound results.

Most rabbitfishes look very much alike in shape and even have similar color patterns. One exception is *Lo vulpinus,* which possesses an elongated snout. Its color pattern is also quite different from those of the other siganids, being a contrasting black and yellow with white markings. All rabbitfishes have the capacity to change color patterns, mostly to a blotched appearance.

Like the surgeonfishes, their diet consists mainly of vegetable items such as algae or higher plants.

Though mostly reef-type fishes, some siganids inhabit brackish water, and at least two species occur in fresh-water.

152. *Siganus virgatus* (Cuvier & Valenciennes). Adult Indo-Pacific Region. The blotchy pattern of the barhead spinefoot in this photograph can be compared with the plain pattern in figure 154. Photo by Dr. Herbert R. Axelrod.

153. *Siganus lineatus* (Cuvier & Valenciennes). 200 mm. Ogasawara Islands. The golden-spot spinefoot have poisonous dorsal fin spines.

154. *Siganus virgatus* (Cuvier & Valenciennes). 40 mm standard length. Okinawa. The barhead spinefoot can change from this typical pattern to a blotchy or barred pattern in a very short time. The characteristic bars on the head remain constant however.

155. *Lo vulpinus* (Schlegel & Müller). 80 mm standard length. Okinawa.

156. *Siganus oramin* (Bloch & Schneider). 100 mm standard length. Aburatsubo, Kanagawa, Japan. The spotted rabbitfish assumes a blotchy appearance when frightened or at night as do other siganids.

Family CANTHIGASTERIDAE
SHARP-NOSED PUFFERS

The sharp-nosed puffers are small fishes that have the ability to inflate themselves (with water or air) into a balloon-like form. Their snout is narrow, pointed and rather long for this type of fish, earning them the common name of sharp-nosed puffers.

They are all small fishes, never reaching a length of over five inches. Their pelvic fins are absent and therefore present no problem when the fish inflates. Movement is carried on mainly by use of the caudal fin, the very small dorsal and anal fins and the pectoral fins. Sharp-nosed puffers can usually be seen hovering over the reef, picking at the small invertebrate animals that constitute most of their diet. These include varied items such as crustaceans of all kinds, molluscs, worms, echinoderms (sea urchins, starfishes, etc.), hydroids and sponges. They also consume algae and marine grasses.

Sharp-nosed puffers are fairly common around the reef, usually swimming in close proximity to some sheltering rock or piece of coral. They do well in aquaria, although they might cause some problems by nipping the fins of more timid fishes.

Their teeth are coalesced into strong, sharp beaks which are necessary to crush the shells of some of their food. If one is not careful when handling these puffers, his fingers might be bitten! These puffers also will nibble at times on the tips of coral branches to get at the polyps or coral animals.

Family DIODONTIDAE
PORCUPINEFISHES

The porcupinefishes also are fishes that can inflate themselves into a round, balloon-like form. They have an added innovation, however, in that their bodies are covered with sharp spines. This provides the potential attacker with both a larger mouthful than anticipated, and a veritable pincushion. Since some of the porcupinefishes grow to a fairly large size (almost two feet in length), it would take a very large predator to swallow such a fish.

In restaurants where the sea is the dominant theme in the decorations, one is likely to see the dried, inflated skin of one of these puffers made into a lamp.

Normally the spines lie close to the body, reducing drag while the fish is swimming. Only when the fish is inflated do the spines become evident. This is the normal occurrence in the genus *Diodon.* A second genus, in this family, *Chilomycterus,* has the spines rigid and always extended. The species of this genus can inflate themselves, but not to the extent of the species of *Diodon.*

Swimming is accomplished in a manner similar to that employed by the trunkfishes and sharp-nosed puffers.

Porcupinefishes possess powerful jaws for crushing hard-shelled animals, and the diet is quite similar to that of the puffers: crustaceans, molluscs, echinoderms and other invertebrates. When attacking a crab which has powerful claws for defense, *Diodon hystrix* will usually grab a claw and twist it off. It will then turn its attention to the other claw, which it promptly removes. When the crab is defenseless, the fish will proceed to finish its meal more leisurely. If the porcupinefish fails to remove both claws, the crab sometimes will use the remaining claw to grab the fish and hold on.

Family TETRAODONTIDAE
PUFFERS

The well-known puffers have the ability to inflate their bodies to such an extent that the fishes are almost circular in shape, with only some fins sticking out from different areas. Normally they swallow water for inflation, but when removed from the water they can use air. In doing so, they make grunting sounds, probably connected with the mechanism of inflation. This capacity to inflate themselves is apparently a protective device that reduces the chances that the predator will be able to swallow them.

As in the sharp-nosed puffers, the pelvic fins are absent. Swimming is accomplished by moving the caudal, pectoral, dorsal and anal fins.

There is a strong parrot-like beak formed from fusion of the teeth. With these beaks the puffers can break up and eat various hard-shelled animals like crustaceans, molluscs and echinoderms. Among the other items of their diet are pieces of coral (polyps) sea squirts, worms and sponges. With this wide variety of food items it is no wonder that they do well in captivity.

Spawning has been reported to occur during spring tides. The males bite and hold on to the tough skin of the females, anchoring themselves to insure proper fertilization of the eggs.

The organs of some species of puffers are poisonous to humans. They contain a deadly poison (tetrodotoxin) which may have been picked up through the foods they eat, as the poison of the surgeonfishes possibly may be picked up, or by some physiological process peculiar to the puffers. In spite of the risk, the flesh is still eaten in some parts of the world, especially Japan, where it is considered a delicacy. When properly prepared, the puffers are safe to eat.

Included in this family are the genera *Arothron, Sphaeroides* and *Tetraodon,* as well as others. Several ichthyologists have combined the family Canthigasteridae with this family.

Family OSTRACIONTIDAE
TRUNKFISHES

Fishes in this family have the scales modified into hard bony plates which have become fused together to form a box-like container, called a carapace, around the fish. Poking out from holes in this carapace are the eyes, snout, gill opening, anus and fins. It is easy to see that these fishes are very poor swimmers, relying on small fins to move the heavy body. The pelvic fins are absent. Although poor swimmers, boxfishes are experts at maneuvering. They can turn easily in small spaces. Fishes of this family are variously known as trunkfishes, cowfishes and boxfishes.

Along with the boxlike armor, some cowfishes have spines extending from various corners or edges of the carapace. At least one species has a spine in the middle of the top of the carapace.

It has been found that some of the cowfishes exude a substance that is poisonous to other fishes and to cowfishes themselves. A boxfish kept in aquaria should not be allowed to be frightened, for it possibly could kill all of the fishes in the tank, including itself. The composition of this toxin is not known.

157. *Canthigaster rivulatus* (Temminck & Schlegel). 60 mm standard length. Kanagawa, Japan. Fully grown specimen.

158. *Canthigaster solandri* Seale. 40 mm standard length. Palau Islands. Solander's sharpnosed puffer is very ornate with blue lines radiating from each eye and spotting on the body. It is wide ranging in the tropical Indo-Pacific and common throughout its range.

159. *Ostracion cubicus* Linnaeus. 80 mm standard length. Kanagawa, Japan. The spotted boxfish is another fish that changes color pattern with age. This and the following five photographs show different aspects of this species.

160. *Ostracion cubicus* Linnaeus. 15 mm standard length. Kanagawa. The juvenile spotted boxfish is bright yellow with spots all over the body. This is the smallest example of the series.

161. *Ostracion cubicus* Linnaeus. 80 mm standard length. Kanagawa. The hard boxlike carapace restricts this fishes movements but serves as a protective device to deter potential predators.

162. *Ostracion cubicus* Linnaeus. 30 mm standard length. This fish is in the process of changing from juvenile to adult color pattern.

163. *Ostracion cubicus* Linnaeus. 20 mm standard length. Okinawa.

164. *Ostracion cubicus* Linnaeus. 30 mm standard length. Okinawa.

165. *Ostracion meleagris* Shaw. 80 mm standard length. Female. Okinawa. White-spotted boxfish.

166. *Lactoria cornuta* (Linnaeus). 40 mm standard length. Kanagawa, Japan. Longhorned cowfish.

167. *Lactoria cornuta* (Linnaeus). 20 mm standard length. Kanagawa, Japan. Longhorned cowfish.

168. *Lactoria fornasina* (Bianconi). 40 mm standard length. Kanagawa, Japan. Thornback cowfish.

169. *Diodon holacanthus* Linnaeus. 40 mm standard length. Okinawa. Spiny puffer.

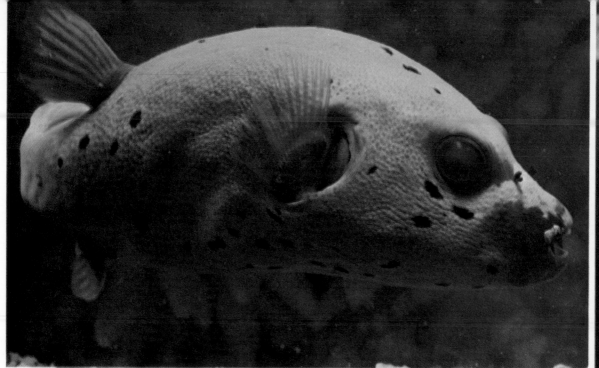

170. *Arothron nigropunctatus* (Schneider). 120 mm standard length. Okinawa. Blackspotted puffer.

171. *Arothron aerostaticus* (Jenyns). 30 mm standard length. Okinawa. Tiger puffer.

172. *Arothron alboreticulatus* (Tanaka). 250 mm standard length. Aburatsubo Marine Park, Japan. Reticulated puffer.

173. *Arothron hispidus* (Linnaeus). 300 mm standard length. Aburatsubo Marine Park, Japan. Striped-belly puffer.

174. *Arothron hispidus* (Linnaeus). 30 mm standard length. Kominato, Chiba, Japan. The color pattern of this juvenile striped-belly puffer can be compared with the adult pattern shown in figure 173.

175. *Arothron hispidus* (Linnaeus). 35 mm standard length. Moroiso, Kanagawa, Japan. The puffers have the ability to inflate themselves with water. This juvenile striped-belly puffer apparently swallowed air and has floated to the surface. It should be able to expel the air and resume its natural position without too much trouble.

176. *Arothron pardalis* (Temminck & Schlegel). 80 mm standard length. Moroiso, Kanagawa, Japan. Japanese puffer.

177. *Arothron pardalis* (Temminck & Schlegel). 200 mm standard length. Moroiso, Kanagawa, Japan.

178. *Arothron hispidus* (Linnaeus). Adult. The striped-belly puffer grows as large as 535 mm. This individual is smaller than the 300 mm adult shown in figure 173. Photo by Dr. D. Terver of the Nancy Aquarium, France.

179. *Arothron stellatus* Bloch & Schneider. Adult. Indo-Pacific. Attains a length of up to 900 mm. Photo by Dr. D. Terver, of the Nancy Aquarium, France.

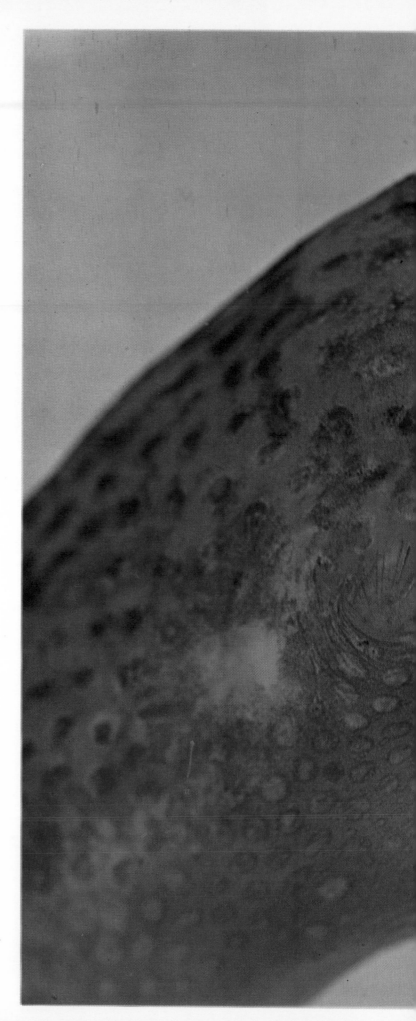

Canthigaster cinctus
70 mm standard length.
Photo by Dr. Herbert R. Axelrod.

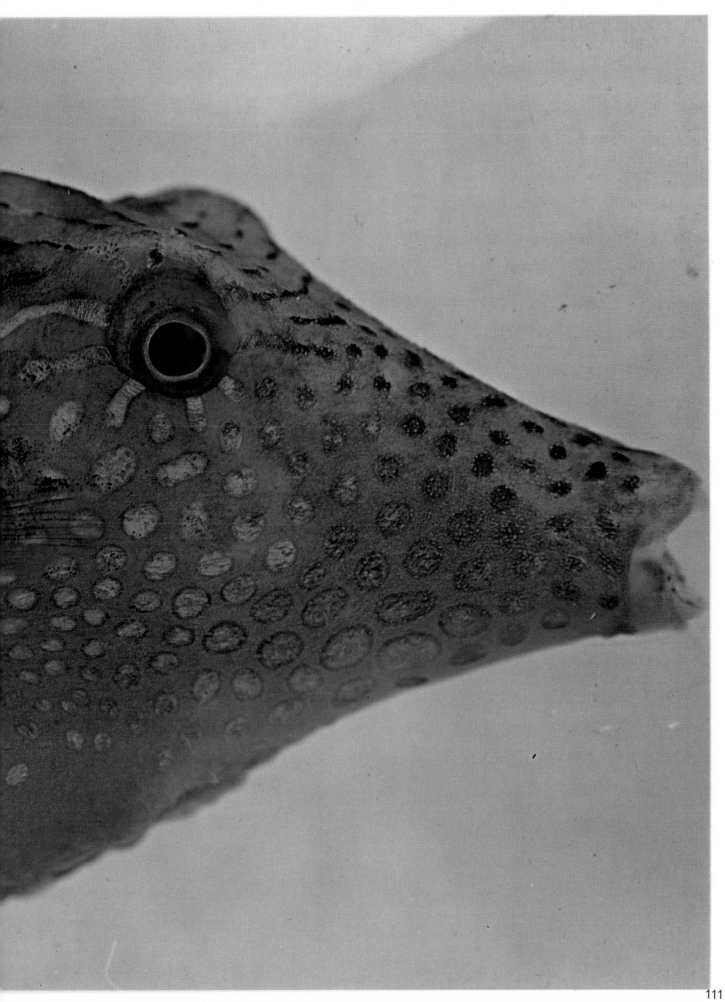

180. *Arothron citrinellus* Günther. Adult. Indo-Pacific. Photo by Dr. D. Terver of the Nancy Aquarium, France.

181. *Arothron meleagris* (Bloch & Schneider). Adult. Indo-Pacific. Photo by Dr. D. Terver of the Nancy Aquarium, France.

182. *Arothron niphobles* (Jordan & Snyder). 80 mm standard length. Moroiso, Kanagawa, Japan. Niphobles puffer.

183. *Arothron hispidus* (Linnaeus). 150 mm standard length. Aburatsubo Marine Park, Japan.

Family BALISTIDAE
TRIGGERFISHES

The triggerfishes are so named because of a peculiar locking mechanism involving the spines of the dorsal fin. Triggerfishes have a large first dorsal spine followed by one or two very small spines. With the posterior spines erect, the strong first dorsal spine is locked into position and cannot be forced into a depressed position without breaking. This mechanism is a protective device which helps the triggerfishes elude capture. When frightened, the triggerfish usually wedges itself into a hole or under a rock and locks its dorsal spine in position. It is difficult to get them out of these holes, although if the posterior spines are depressed the anterior spine will easily fold back and the fish can be retrieved.

The body is covered with osseous scales, fitting closely together and forming a flexible armor. Unlike the previous groups of plectognaths (a term referring to the various families of puffers, boxfishes, triggerfishes, etc.) the triggerfishes are quite mobile, though not especially fast swimmers. Swimming is accomplished mainly by use of the second dorsal fin and the anal fin, with the pectoral fins as secondary propulsive units. The caudal fin, a prime driving force in other fishes, is used mainly as a rudder in the triggerfishes.

When triggerfishes are removed from the water, grunting noises can be heard. This is basically produced by vibrations of the swim bladder. What use these sounds serve underwater is still not completely known.

Triggerfishes have well-defined teeth, in contrast to the previous families in which the teeth are coalesced into beaks or otherwise modified. The upper jaw contains a second row of flattened, plate-like teeth behind the outer row of eight teeth. The diet of these fishes is similar to that of the other plectognaths; they eat crustaceans, molluscs and echinoderms. Triggerfishes are among the few fishes able to cope with the long, dangerous spines of the black sea urchin. Protected by the hard platelike scales, they bite the spines off or grab a spine and turn the animal upside down, thus exposing the vulnerable soft underside of the urchin.

Some of the triggerfishes are also involved in cases of food poisoning.

Many of the triggerfishes are very attractively patterned. They are considered good aquarium fishes; some species, such as the clown triggerfish, *Balistoides niger*, command a very high price in the commercial trade. Triggerfishes are considered 'personality' fishes, being easily trained to do tricks and to eat from their owners' fingers. The triggerfishes have strong jaws with which to crush the shells of food, so they can also do a lot of damage to a person's fingers. These fishes were once referred to as the "piranhas of the sea."

It is in this family that the famous Hawaiian triggerfish, the humuhumunuku-nuku-a-puaa, is found.

Most of the triggerfishes are found on coral reefs in relatively shallow water. The juveniles sometimes can be found around floating sea-weeds such as *Sargassum,* as can an occasional adult as well. On the reef they live in caves or holes which they excavate themselves. The excavating process is accomplished by a sucking process,

184. *Oxymonacanthus longirostris* (Bloch & Schneider). 73 mm standard length. Indo-Pacific. Photo by Dr. John E. Randall.

185. *Balistoides niger* (Bonnaterre). Adult. Indo-Pacific. Clown triggerfish. Photo by Hans & Klaus Paysan.

186. *Balistoides niger* (Bonnaterre). 200 mm standard length. Okinawa. Clown triggerfish.

187. *Rhinecanthus aculeatus* (Linnaeus). 120 mm standard length. Okinawa. Humu-humu-nuku-nuku-a-puaa (Hawaiian).

188. *Pseudobalistes fuscus* (Bloch & Schneider). 25 mm standard length. Moroiso, Kanagawa, Japan. Decorated triggerfish.

189. *Rhinecanthus rectangulus (Bloch & Schneider).* 40 mm standard length. Okinawa. Rectangle triggerfish.

190. *Pervagor melanocephalus* (Bleeker). 60 mm standard length. Okinawa. Lace-finned filefish.

191. *Melichthys vidua* (Solander). 150 mm standard length. Okinawa. Pink-tailed triggerfish.

192. *Xanthichthys mento* (Jordan & Gilbert). 150 mm standard length. Adult male. Aburatsubo Marine Park, Japan. Crosshatch triggerfish.

193. *Odonus niger* (Rüppell). 70 mm standard length. Okinawa. Red-toothed triggerfish.

194. *Balistapus undulatus* (Park). 70 mm standard length. Okinawa. Undulate triggerfish.

195. *Sufflamen* sp. 40 mm. Okinawa. This unidentified
species turns brown with age.

196. *Sufflamen chrysoptera* Schneider. 120 mm.
Okinawa. White-rim triggerfish.

197. *Canthidermis maculatus* (Bloch). 30 mm. Kanagawa, Japan. Spotted triggerfish.

198. *Melichthys vidua* (Solander). 70 mm. Okinawa.
Pink-tailed triggerfish.

199. *Sufflamen fraenatus* Richardson. 200 mm.
Okinawa.

200. *Meuschenia skottowei* Whitley. Subadult. Pacific coast of Australia. Photo by Dr. Herbert R. Axelrod.

201. *Meuschenia skottowei* Whitley. Adult. Pacific coast of Australia. Photo by Dr. Herbert R. Axelrod.

the sand being expelled through the gill openings. Larger items are moved with the strong jaws.

The caudal peduncle is provided with various spines which come into play when triggerfishes do battle. They engage in "tail-slapping," a lateral motion of the tail against an opponent. Triggerfishes are very aggressive fishes, apparently ready to attack all comers.

It has been said that triggerfishes chase other fishes, directing their attack at the vulnerable eyes, which they can expertly extricate. It is no wonder that many of the reef inhabitants have color patterns which render the eyes difficult to see!

Family MONACANTHIDAE
FILEFISHES

The filefishes are very closely related to the triggerfishes and have occasionally been placed in the same family. The main difference that can be noticed is that the filefishes have a single long dorsal fin spine followed by a second, rudimentary spine. In addition, filefishes have a body covering which is rough or velvety, and not like the hard, bony plate-like scales of the triggerfishes.

Locomotion is similar to that in the triggerfishes, although the caudal fin plays a more active role in propulsion. The jaws have six sharp teeth. In the upper jaw there is an additional inner row of four teeth.

Filefishes eat a wide variety of food items, including such unusual items as sponges, corals (including stinging coral), hydroids and algae, as well as the usual diet of small worms, crustaceans and molluscs.

Filefishes can usually be found hiding among the various plants or attached animals, such as sea fans or sea whips, on the reef.

They are also a constant member of the floating *Sargassum* community, well hidden among the fronds of this algae by their brownish to orange coloration and various tabs of skin imitating the construction of the weed. One species at least, *Oxymonacanthus longirostris,* is a reef filefish, occuring in the branches of various species of corals. This species is brightly colored, in contrast to most other species of filefishes, being green with large orange spots. Its snout is elongate, perhaps as an adaptation to living among coral, where small animals hide in the interstices or small crevices. When frightened it wedges itself deeply into the forks of the branches and is very difficult to dislodge.

Differences between the sexes are present in the form of color markings, body proportions and in the development of spines or bristles on the caudal peducle. These are either absent in the females or, when present in both sexes, are better developed in the male.

Alutera scripta, a species from the tropical areas of the world, is perhaps the largest filefish, reported to reach a length of some 40 inches.

Balistoides niger (Bonnaterre). Adult. Indo-Pacific. Clown triggerfish. Photo by Hans & Klaus Paysan.

202. *Balistapus undulatus* (Park). Indo-Pacific. This young individual of the undulate triggerfish differs slightly from the adult as seen below in figure 203. Photo of a Philippine specimen by Earl Kennedy.

203. *Balistapus undulatus* (Park). Adult. Indo-Pacific. Undulate triggerfish. Photo by Hans & Klaus Paysan.

204. *Rhinecanthus verrucosus* (L.) 70 mm standard length. Okinawa. Black-bellied triggerfish.

205. *Pseudobalistes fuscus* (Bloch & Schneider). 200 mm standard length. Okinawa. The juvenile pattern of this species is indicated in fig. 188. There also is a distinct subadult pattern.

206. *Alutera monoceros* (Linnaeus). 80 mm standard length. Aburatsubo, Kanagawa, Japan. Unicorn leather-jacket.

207. *Paramonacanthus oblongus* (Temminck & Schlegel). 30 mm. Shimoda, Shizuoka, Japan. Oblong filefish.

208. *Navodon modestus* (Günther). 100 mm. Aburatsubo, Kanagawa, Japan. Blotched filefish.

209. *Rudarius ércodes* Jordan & Fowler. 35 mm. Aburatsubo, Kanagawa, Japan. Network filefish.

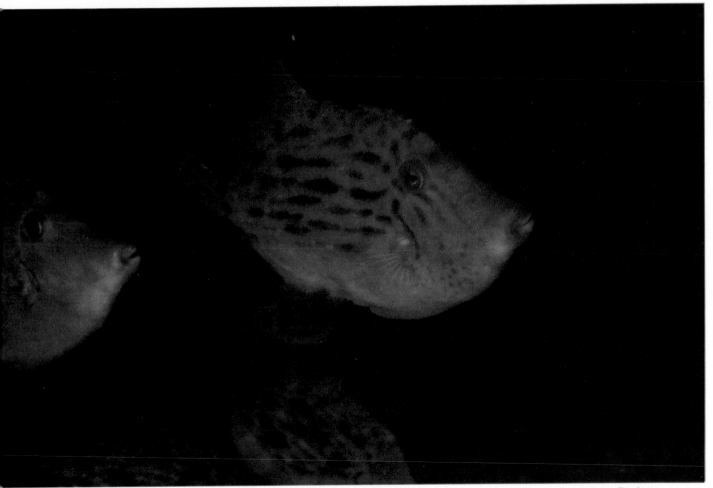

210. *Stephanolepis cirrhifer* (Temminck & Schlegel). 100 mm. Aburatsubo, Kanagawa, Japan. Porky.

Family LABRIDAE
WRASSES

The wrasses are a large and complicated group of fishes found in tropical and temperate waters. They are one of the largest families of fishes in both numbers and in size, ranging from the small three-inch species of the genus *Labroides* to the very large members of the genus *Cheilinus,* which reach a length of ten feet and a weight of several hundred pounds.

The basic shape of wrasses is elongate, compressed, with continuous dorsal and anal fins, but there are many variations from this pattern. The lips are thickened; the teeth are separate and strong, usually with some projecting, giving the fishes a buck-tooth appearence.

The color patterns of the wrasses are among the most brilliant on the coral reefs. Complicating matters, however, is the problem wherein juvenile wrasses are differently colored from the adults in many species, and the males may have different color patterns from the females. In some species there may be three different color patterns. More normal is the occurrence of special males which grow larger than the other males and females and take on a color pattern all their own. These are easily recognized as males, whereas the others are too similarly colored to distinguish the sexes. These special males may be the result of sex reversal, wherein the female changes physiologically into a male and assumes a distinctive color pattern.

Most of the wrasses eat small invertebrates and fishes. Crustaceans and molluscs are crushed with specially constructed pharyngeal teeth.

Wrasses are generally non-schooling fishes that swim around the reef searching for food. At the time of spawning, they aggregate in moderate numbers and mill around in the vicinity of some prominent coral or rocky formation. At some signal a small group of them will leave the general aggregation and swim up in the water a short distance, where eggs and sperm are released. The motion of the fishes in the vicinity of this release of sexual products ensures fertilization. The group then returns to the others, and the activity is performed by others of the aggregation at short intervals. These group spawning individuals are all similarly colored. A second type of spawning occurs, involving the special males mentioned above. A single male will spawn with a single female rather than in a group. The actual spawning activity is similar to that of the group spawners.

Wrasses generally use their pectoral fins for most of the swimming done around the reef. When extra speed is needed, the caudal fin is brought into play. This reef cruising usually occurs during the day. At night time these fishes have a peculiar sleeping behavior. Some species dive into the sand and remain there all night. Others secrete a mucous cocoon in which they sleep.

When frightened, the wrasses revert to flight in some cases, as do other fishes, but usually they disappear into a sandy patch. *Labroides* species have been reported to "hide" by constructing a cocoon. Unless this cocoon is toxic or in some way disagreeable to the predator, it does not appear to afford much protection.

The genus *Labroides* has gained much prominence in the last twenty years since the discovery of its cleaning habits, probably one of the great breakthroughs in the study of fish behavior. Fishes of the genus *Labroides* are called cleaner wrasses because the major part of their diet consists of parasites of other fishes. A sort of mutual understanding has evolved between the cleaner wrasses and other fishes, in which fishes infested with parasites will assume very still (sometimes awkward) positions while the small wrasses cover almost every inch of their bodies searching for food. Although the fishes that come for this service are large enough to easily eat the cleaner, they normally will not do so, even if the cleaner enters the mouth and gill regions. Sometimes the cleaners get a little over-enthusiastic in their nibblings, and the fish being cleaned will give a sudden start; usually, however, it soon returns to its pose. The cleaner wrasses usually have a certain territory in which they remain month after month, servicing fishes that come there. Some fishes have been seen returning day after day to the same cleaning station to be rid of their ectoparasites. If the cleaners are removed from a particular location, the fishes seem to become heavily infested with parasites; sores or ragged fins develop. Other wrasses, particularly juveniles, engage in cleaning, but only on a part-time basis.

The bird wrasse, *Gomphosus varius,* is a peculiarly shaped wrasse in which the snout has become elongate and arched slightly downward. Although two species were once thought to exist, it appears that there is only a single species with two distinct color patterns, male and female, and some geographic variation.

Although wrasses are colorful, they usually do not make good aquarium species. They are aggressive and cause considerable damage to the other aquarium fishes. During the initial stages of aquarium life, however, they are timid and for the first week or so will not be seen, spending much of the time beneath the sand.

Labroides dimidiatus. Okinawa. This is the famous cleaner wrasse that removes parasites from the bodies of other fishes.

Photo by G. Marcuse

211. Unidentified wrasse, possibly the young form of *Bodianus oxycephalus* (Bleeker). About 60 mm standard length. Izu Marine Park, Japan.

212. *Pseudolabrus gracilis* (Steindachner). 80 mm standard length. Izu Marine Park, Japan. Brownstripe wrasse.

213. *Pseudolabrus japonicus* (Houttuyn). 130 mm standard length. Aburatsubo, Kanagawa, Japan. Japanese Wrasse.

214. *Bodianus diana*
Lacépède). 130 mm standard length. Okinawa. Diana wrasse.

215. *Stethojulis axillaris*
(Quoy & Gaimard). 70 mm standard length. Okinawa. Male Red-shoulder wrasse or speckled wrasse (the latter name more aptly applied to the female of this species shown in figure 255).

216. *Bodianus mesothorax*
(Schneider). Subadult. Ueno Zoo Aquarium, Japan. Black-belt wrasse.

217. *Pteragogus* sp. Izu Marine Park, Japan. Probably the young form of *Pteragogus flagellifera*. (See figure 258.)

218. *Iniistius pavo* (Cuvier & Valenciennes). 30 mm standard length. Izu Marine Park, Japan. Unicorn Razorfish.

219. *Choerodon* sp. 30 mm standard length. Izu Marine Park, Japan. Possibly the young form of *Choerodon schoenleinii* (Valenciennes).

220. *Julis musume* Jordan & Snyder. 70 mm standard length. Izu Marine Park, Japan. This red-striped wrasse has buried itself in the sand possibly to avoid some danger. This is common behavior in the wrasse family.

221. *Bodianus oxycephalus* (Bleeker). Shimoda, Shizuoka, Japan. The young of this species might be the fish depicted in figure 211.

222. *Thalassoma amblycephalus* (Bleeker). 80 mm standard length. Okinawa. Paddlefin wrasse.

223. *Thalassoma amblycephalus* (Bleeker). 60 mm standard length. Okinawa. Rainbow wrasse.

224. *Stethojulis kalosoma* (Bleeker). 80 mm standard length. Aburatsubo, Kanagawa, Japan. One-line rainbow wrasse.

225. *Stethojulis kalosoma* (Bleeker). 80 mm standard length. Aburatsubo, Kanagawa, Japan. The one-line rainbow wrasse has attempted to cover itself with the gravel from the bottom.

226. *Malacanthus latovittatus* (Lacépède). 180 mm. Aburatsubo, Kanagawa, Japan.

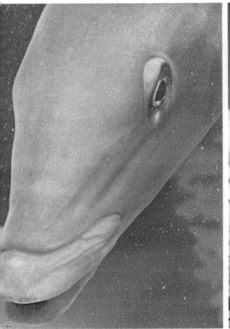

227. *Malacanthus latovittatus* (Lacépède). 180 mm standard length. Aburatsubo, Kanagawa, Japan. Blue whiting (family Branchiostegidae).

228. Underwater photograph of an unidentified juvenile wrasse. Estimated size about 30 mm standard length. Moroiso, Kanagawa, Japan.

229. *Labroides dimidiatus* (Cuvier & Valenciennes). 40 mm standard length. Okinawa.

230. *Labroides bicolor* Fowler & Bean. 60 mm standard length. Okinawa. The bicolor cleaner wrasse also is a well known parasite remover.

231. *Halichoeres poecilopterus* (Temminck & Schlegel). 130 mm standard length. Moroiso, Kanagawa, Japan. This is the adult male color pattern of the peacock wrasse.

232. *Halichoeres poecilopterus* (Temminck & Schlegel). About 130 mm standard length. Moroiso, Kanagawa, Japan. The adult female peacock wrasse with a different color pattern than that of the male shown above (fig. 231).

233. *Coris yama-shiroi* (Schmidt). 80 mm standard length. Okinawa. Blushing wrasse.

234. *Semicossyphus reticulatus* (Valenciennes). 40 mm standard length. Izu Marine Park, Japan. Juvenile stage.

235. *Semicossyphus reticulatus* (Valenciennes). 60 mm standard length. Izu Marine Park, Japan. Slightly older juvenile.

236. *Semicossyphus reticulatus* (Valenciennes). 800 mm standard length. Enoshima Aquarium, Japan. Old adult.

237. *Semicossyphus reticulatus* (Valenciennes). 300 mm standard length. Shimoda, Shizuoka, Japan. Adult. Cold porgy.

238. *Coris gaimard* (Quoy & Gaimard). 30 mm standard length. Okinawa. The clown wrasse undergoes a complete change of color pattern shown in the next two photographs (figs. 239 and 240).

239. *Coris gaimard* (Quoy & Gaimard). 60 mm standard length. Okinawa. The intermediate stage in which remnants of the juvenile color pattern are still noticeable.

240. *Coris gaimard* (Quoy & Gaimard). 150 mm standard length. Okinawa. Adult fish completely transformed.

140

241. *Coris aygula* Lacépède. 30 mm standard length. Okinawa. Juvenile. Twinspot wrasse.

242. *Coris aygula* Lacépède. 80 mm standard length. Okinawa. Subadult twinspot wrasse.

243. *Anampses* sp. About 80 mm standard length. Ueno Zoo Aquarium, Japan.

244. *Gomphosus varius* Lacépède. 60 mm standard length. Zushi, Kanagawa, Japan. Bird wrasse. Male.

245. *Gomphosus varius*
Lacépède. 60 mm standard
length. Okinawa. The adult
female bird wrasse is quite
different from the adult male
(fig. 244).

246. *Bodianus bilunulatus*
(Lacépède). 300 mm standard
length. Ogasawara Islands,
Japan. The adult Pacific
Hogfish shown here has a
different color pattern from
the juvenile (not
shown).

247. *Halichoeres marginatus*
Rüppell. 25 mm standard
length. Okinawa.

248. *Anampses caeruleopunctatus* Rüppell. 50 mm standard length. Izu Marine Park, Japan. This young blue-spotted wrasse can be compared to the adult coloration in figure 251.

249. Unidentified wrasse about 30 mm standard length. This wrasse could be the earlier juvenile stage of *Anampses caeruleopunctatus,* older individuals being depicted in figures 248 and 251. Okinawa.

250. *Hemigymnus fasciatus* (Bloch). 130 mm standard length. Okinawa. Banded wrasse.

251. *Anampses caeruleopunctatus* Rüppell. 60 mm standard length. Izu Marine Park, Japan. Adult color phase.

252. *Hemigymnus melapterus* (Bloch). 100 mm standard length. Okinawa. The color changes that this wrasse goes through with growth are still not fully understood. Half-and-half wrasse.

253. *Hologymnosus semidiscus* (Lacépède). 100 mm standard length. Okinawa. The vertical stripes on this fish can disappear leaving only the horizontal stripes.

254. *Thalassoma hardwickei* (Bennett). 130 mm standard length. Okinawa. Hardwicke's wrasse.

255. *Stethojulis axillaris* (Quoy & Gaimard). 80 mm standard length. Okinawa. Female (see fig. 215 for male's colors).

256. *Cheilinus bimaculatus* Valenciennes. 80 mm standard length. Izu Marine Park, Japan. Ceram wrasse.

257. *Halichoeres hortulanus* (Lacépède). 30 mm standard length. Okinawa. Checkerboard wrasse.

258. *Pteragogus flagellifera* (Cuvier & Valenciennes). 90 mm standard length. Aburatsubo, Kanagawa, Japan.

259. *Thalassoma lutescens* (Lay & Bennett). 90 mm standard length. Okinawa. Adult female.

260. Unidentified species of wrasse possibly in the genus *Choerodon.* Approximately 60 mm standard length. Izu Marine Park, Japan.

261. *Thalassoma lutescens* (Lay & Bennett). 70 mm standard length. Okinawa. The adult male shown here can be compared with the female in figure 259.

262. *Xyrichthys taeniourus* (Lacépède). 120 mm standard length. Okinawa. This fish was also known under the name of *Novaculichthys taeniourus.* Pearl-scale razorfish.

263. *Choerodon azurio* (Jordan & Snyder). 130 mm standard length. Aburatsubo, Kanagawa, Japan. Tawny wrasse.

264. *Choerodon azurio* (Jordan & Snyder). 130 mm standard length. Aburatsubo, Kanagawa, Japan. Frontal view showing separate, enlarged canine teeth typical of the wrasse family.

Family SCARIDAE
PARROTFISHES

Parrotfishes closely resemble the wrasses, although they do not have the variety of different shapes that can be found among the wrasses. The major difference is in the structure of the teeth, which are fused into large, strong, parrot-like beaks. In addition, they have specially constructed pharyngeal teeth for crushing the shells or skeletons of various animals.

On the reef one can hear the crunching and gnawing sounds these fishes make as they chew off bits of the coral branches. These fishes have become one of the chief sources of coral reef erosion. The coral is ground very finely in the pharyngeal mill and passed through the intestine of the fish. The nutritive material is digested, and the coral debris is passed out and returned to the reef. Much of the food ingested is various types of algae.

The parrotfishes move over the reefs in fairly large schools, browsing as they go, earning them their reputation as cattle of the sea. Sometimes these schools can be seen in water so shallow that the dorsal fin and part of the back are exposed. Some of the parrotfishes create mounds of ground-up coral, since they defecate in the same place time after time.

Since most parrotfishes are very similar in form, color pattern is used to distinguish the species. This has caused many problems, because there is more than one color pattern for each species. The two different color patterns belong to the juveniles, females and some males on the one hand, and special males on the other, much as in the wrasses. Some species have three patterns, the juveniles and adults being different, and special males having yet another pattern.

Spawning occurs in groups and as pairs of special males and single females, as described under the family Labridae. The brightest, gaudiest colors always belong to the large, special males.

Studies on the homing behavior of parrotfishes have been made. It was found that the parrotfishes would leave their home territory, usually a cave, during the day to forage on the reef some distance away. In the evening they were always able to return to the same cave that they left in the morning. The theory is that they can tell direction by the angle of the sun.

At night some parrotfishes normally secrete a mucous cocoon and sleep on the bottom or on the rocks of the reef. The cocoon is transparent and difficult to see unless covered by some silt. The envelope takes some thirty minutes to be constructed. The reason for the envelope is still not known. When a sleeping parrotfish is awakened at night, it appears uncoordinated for a time, bumping into objects as it swims awkwardly away. Eventually, when the disturbing influence passes, the parrotfish will settle down on the reef again and go back to sleep. The parrotfishes sleep so soundly that if a diver lifts them up very carefully they can be removed from the reef without being awakened.

Parrotfishes are fairly large fishes, the smallest being about a foot and a half in length, the largest normally reaching about six feet in length. Of course, as in the case of many fishes, reports of gigantic individuals set the largest size far beyond the normal length. In the case of the parrotfishes, records of twelve-foot monsters have appeared. With the great advances in skin diving, it is certain that record fishes have been seen that have avoided capture so far. Unfortunately, it is extremely difficult to authenticate these sight records.

Large males of some parrotfish species develop a large prominent forehead and are usually referred to as bumphead males.

265. *Scarus sexvittatus* Rüppell. 325 mm standard length. Adult male from Eniwetok, Marshall Islands. Photo by Dr. John E. Randall.

266. *Scarus sexvittatus* Rüppell. 172 mm standard length. Adult female from Tahiti. Photo by Dr. John E. Randall.

267. *Scarus* sp. (possibly *Scarus ghobban,* see fig. 269). 120 mm standard length. Okinawa.

268. *Scarus* sp. (possibly *Scarus ghobban,* see fig. 269). 120 mm standard length. Okinawa. This frontal view shows the coalesced teeth forming the "beak" of parrotfishes.

269. *Scarus ghobban*
Forskål. 200 mm
standard length.
Ogasawara Islands,
Japan. Blue-trim
parrotfish.

270. *Scarus microrhinos*
Bleeker. 417 mm
standard length. Male
specimen from Tahiti
exhibiting the enlarged
"nose" found in many
adult males. Photo by
Dr. John E. Randall.

271. *Bolbometapon bicolor*
(Rüppell). 40 mm
standard length.
Okinawa. Bicolored
parrotfish.

Family CIRRHITIDAE

HAWKFISHES

Hawkfishes are similar in appearance to the scorpionfishes, family Scorpaenidae, but lack the head spines of those fishes. Hawkfishes have large pectoral fins with characteristically thickened simple rays. In addition, cirrhitids are distincitve in possessing a fringe at the back of the anterior nostril.

The large pectoral fins aid these fishes in perching on the tops of coral heads in a manner similar to hawks waiting on a high perch for their prey. The enlarged rays act as supports for hanging onto the rough surface. When danger threatens, their perches become refuges as they disappear into the coral branches. When a section of coral containing hawkfishes is removed from the water, the hawkfishes remain with the coral for some time before eventually having to wiggle out and drop back into the water.

Small fishes and crustaceans constitute the main ingredients in the hawkfishes' diets. They are captured by sudden dashes from the coral resting place of the hawkfish.

In the genus *Paracirrhites* several species have a brightly colored marking extending upward and backward from the eye. It would seem unusual for a color pattern to direct attention, via brightness, to as vulnerable an organ as an eye. It must for the moment remain one of the unexplainable curiosities of nature.

In the genus *Amblycirrhitus* there is a tuft of cirri present on the tip of each dorsal fin spine; the color pattern is basically pale with darker markings.

Probably the most unusual hawkfish is *Oxycirrhites typus*. Its snout has evolved into an elongate structure, just as has happened in so many other families of reef fishes.

272. *Paracirrhites arcatus* (Cuvier & Valenciennes). 60 mm standard length. Eniwetok, Marshall Islands. Photo by Dr. John E. Randall.

273. *Labracinus cyclophthalmus* (Müller & Troschel). Adult male. Philippine Islands. Photo by Earl Kennedy.

Family PSEUDOCHROMIDAE

DOTTYBACKS

The pseudochromids, or dottybacks as they are commonly called, are small fishes inhabiting coastal waters and coral reefs. Many species are brightly colored and have become popular aquarium fishes.

The body is elongate and compressed, with long, continuous dorsal fins. They have often been included with the groupers, family Serranidae, but are distinguished by their interrupted lateral line; that is, the lateral line is in two separate sections, one along the back, the other on the caudal peduncle. The dorsal fin usually contains only three slender spines and numerous rays, although exceptions do occur.

There are few species in this family, most of which fall into the two genera *Labracinus* and *Pseudochromis*. It has been discovered by Dr. L. P. Schultz that sexes can be distinguished on the basis of certain aspects of the color pattern. In *Labracinus cyclophthalmus,* which is represented in the color photographs, males have black spots or blotches on the base of the dorsal fin membranes, usually between dorsal rays number five and ten. Females, on the other hand, have comma-shaped marks in the dorsal fin.

The closely related family Plesiopidae is more grouper-like but, like the dottybacks, still retains the distinguishing feature of two lateral lines. *Calloplesiops altivelis,* well known to marine aquarists as the comet, is quite distinctive, with blue-white spotting on a blackish-brown background. Its great beauty and interesting fin formation make this a fish very much in demand.

274. *Labracinus cyclophthalmus* (Müller & Troschel). 100 mm standard length. Okinawa. Adult female. The pattern of black markings in the dorsal fins of this species is used to distinguish the sexes according to Dr. L. P. Schultz.

275. *Cirrhitichthys aprinus* (Cuvier). 60 mm standard length. Okinawa. Spotted hawkfish. The tasseled appearance of the dorsal fin spines are evident in this photo.

276. *Paracirrhites forsteri* (Bloch & Schneider). 120 mm standard length. Okinawa. Freckled hawkfish.

277. *Cirrhitichthys aureus* (Temminck & Schlegel). 50 mm standard length. Izu Marine Park, Japan. Golden hawkfish.

278. *Cirrhitichthys oxycephalus* (Bleeker). About 40 mm standard length. Palau Islands. Photo by Dr. John E. Randall.

Family BLENNIIDAE

BLENNIES

The name blenny is applied to several different families of fishes, most important of which are the scaled blennies (family Clinidae) and the naked or scaleless blennies, belonging to the family Blenniidae.

The scaleless blennies are small fishes usually less than four inches in length. They usually possess simple to ornate cirri or fleshy crests on the head. The dorsal fin may be continuous, notched, or sometimes completely divided. The spines contained in these fins are flexible, slender, and usually fewer in number than the rays of the dorsal fin. The pelvic fins have a reduced number of rays (2-4).

There are about 300 scaleless blennies according to Dr. V. G. Springer, the authority on these fishes. They are found in most oceans of the tropical and temperate regions but become scarce in the colder waters. They prefer areas where there are hiding places such as coral or rocks.

Most blennies are bottom fishes commonly seen lying with their tails curled in an arc. When disturbed they make a hasty retreat to the shelter of nearby rocks. The curled tail might give them an initial thrust in this flight. Some blennies have their gill openings reduced to small slits, their breathing apparatus providing a pumping action resulting in the expulsion of jets of water that may assist in swimming motions.

Blennies have a wide variety of feeding habits, as may be expected in such a large family. Some are carnivores and some herbivores, a number of the carnivores adopting peculiar behavioral habits. Species of the genus *Meiacanthus*, for example, have special enlarged canine teeth in the lower jaw; these teeth are provided with poison glands and can inflict a painful wound even in humans. With this weapon, the species of *Meiacanthus* are not vicious predators, but eat mainly annelid worms. They are not totally sedentary, as are most other blennies, but spend some of their time swimming. Such active swimming is accomplished with the aid of a swimbladder, an organ absent in other blennies.

The mimic blenny, *Aspidontus taeniatus,* bears a startling resemblance to the cleaner wrasse *Labroides dimidiatus.* A fish that poses to be cleaned by the 'wrasse' usually loses a piece of flesh to the mimic. But fishes are able to learn and soon are able to distinguish which is the true cleaner and which is the dangerous species.

Differences between the sexes are not easily detected. In females the first of two anal spines is buried in tissues, but there are knob-like fleshy proturberances on these spines in mature males. Eggs are placed in nests and guarded by the male. Some larvae are pelagic and go through a larval stage so different in appearance from the adults that it received a new name, *ophioblennius,* which is still retained as a general term for these larvae. Blennies collected in the plankton in Hawaii by one of the authors (WEB) were mostly transparent, although a silver color hid the internal organs. After being placed in small aquaria they started to change color, becoming mottled brownish. The change took several days to be completed.

Blennies are territorial fishes and will protect their areas vigorously. They will select a particular spot in a tank to set up housekeeping and guard it against fishes larger than themselves. Several blennies placed in an aquarium with only a few good holes that could be used for nesting areas will constantly fight over the choice locations, the weaker blennies eventually becoming damaged from such squabbling.

Many blennies are beautifully patterned and have bright colors. It is surprising that aquarists have not shown much more interest in these fishes.

279. *Plagiotremus rhinorhynchos* (Bleeker). About 50 mm standard length. Palau Islands. Photo by Dr. John E. Randall.

280. *Plagiotremus rhinorhynchos* (Bleeker). 50 mm standard length. Moroiso, Kanagawa, Japan. Sabre-toothed blenny.

281. *Zoarchias veneficus* Jordan & Snyder. 50 mm standard length. Shimoda, Shizuoka, Japan.

282. *Tripterygion etheostoma* Jordan & Snyder. 40 mm standard length. Moroiso, Kanagawa, Japan. Adult.

283. *Omobranchus elegans* (Steindachner). Female, 50 mm standard length. Kamakura, Kanagawa, Japan.

284. *Neoclinus bryope* (Jordan & Snyder). 60 mm standard length. Moroiso, Kanagawa, Japan. Crowned blenny.

285. *Neoclinus bryope* (Jordan & Snyder). 60 mm standard length. Moroiso, Kanagawa, Japan. The common name "crowned blenny" was derived from the appearance of the fringed tentacles crowning the top of the head.

286. *Meiacanthus atrodorsalis* (Günther). 60 mm standard length. Amami-Oshima Islands. The length of the black stripe in the dorsal fin of the forktail blenny is highly variable.

287. *Pholidichthys leucotaenia* Bleeker. 60 mm standard length. Philippine Islands.

288. *Meiacanthus kamohorai* (Valenciennes). 50 mm standard length. Okinawa. Black-and-white striped blenny.

289. *Petroscirtes breviceps*. 50 mm standard length. Aburatsubo. Kanagawa, Japan. Brown-striped blenny.

290. *Aspasmichthys ciconae* (Jordan & Fowler). 30 mm standard length. Aburatsubo, Kanagawa, Japan. Golden clingfish.

291. *Lepadichthys frenatus* Waite. 30 mm standard length. Aburatsubo Marine Park, Japan. Green clingfish.

292.　*Parapercis multifasciatus* (Döderlein). 50 mm. Izu Marine Park. Barred perch.

293.　*Pseudoblennius cottoides* (Richardson). 70 mm. Moroiso, Kanagawa, Japan. Painted blenny.

294.　*Pseudoblennius percoides* Günther. 80 mm. Moroiso, Kanagawa, Japan. Thick-lipped blenny.

295. *Parapercis sexfasciatus* (Temminck & Schlegel). 60 mm standard length. Aburatsubo, Kanagawa, Japan. Six-banded perch.

296. Unknown species of sea snail, family Liparidae, about 20 mm standard length. Shimoda, Shizuoka, Japan.

297. *Blennius yatabei* (Jordan & Snyder). About 40 mm standard length. Male and female from Shimoda, Shizuoka, Japan.

298. *Tripterygion bapturum* Jordan & Snyder. 40 mm standard length. Izu Marine Park, Japan. Blue-faced blenny.

299. *Lotella maximowiczi* Herzenstein. 80 mm standard length. Shimoda, Shizuoka, Japan. Max's cod.

300. *Dictyosoma burgeri* Van der Hoeven. 60 mm standard length. Shimoda, Shizuoka, Japan. Skunk blenny.

301. *Eleotroides virgata* (Temminck & Schlegel). 60 mm standard length. Izu Marine Park, Japan. Blue-line goby.

Family GOBIIDAE
GOBIES

The catch-all name goby includes a large number of fishes usually divided into several families of which Gobiidae is the largest and most important. Of the 600 or so gobies, more than half are contained in this family. Other goby-type fishes include the sleeper gobies (Eleotridae), loach gobies (Microdesmidae), and others.

Gobies, as represented in the family Gobiidae, are small, usually less than four inches in length. The smallest recorded vertebrate is a goby from the Philippine Islands which when fully grown attains a length of only 6 mm. It occurs in freshwater lakes and streams.

The most typical characteristic of the gobies is that the pelvic fins are fused together to form a sucking disc with which the fish can maintain itself on a substrate in a fairly strong current. There are usually two dorsal fins, the gobies lack the elaborate cirri of the blennies. The lateral line is absent. Like the bottom-dwelling blennies, the gobies also lack a swim bladder.

Being primarily bottom fishes, the gobies have invaded many niches in the available habitats. In some cases they have entered into commensal relationships with other animals. Several different species live with crustaceans in burrows constructed by these crustaceans. The crustaceans, usually snapping shrimp, continue to keep the burrow in good repair, thus providing a home for the fish while the fish usually warn the shrimp when danger threatens.

At least one group of fishes within the family is able to leave the water for short periods of time. Generally called mudskippers, *(Periophthalmus, Boleophthalmus)*, they remain behind on the mudflats or in mangrove swamps when the water recedes. They are not harmed by their lack of submergence as long as the gills and parts of their bodies remain moist. Mudskippers are named for their ability to 'skip' over the mud-flats very rapidly, making their capture difficult.

Species of the genus *Gobiodon* and their relatives make their home in the branches of coral. In some cases they may share a coral head with fishes like hawkfishes, scorpionfishes, damselfishes, and others. These gobies lay their eggs in the angle of the coral branches, with several pairs often spawning in the same coral head.

The goby egg is typically elongate and is firmly attached to some part of the substrate, whether it be grass, rock, coral, or parts of the burrow. The parents usually guard the nest until the eggs hatch. Some of the gobies have pelagic larvae which are mostly silver and transparent, with .an oil globule in the visceral area, probably as an aid to flotation.

While most gobies are rather drably colored, some have just as brilliant colors as many reef fishes. One species of goby, *Ptereleotris splendidus,* is bright red and white, a spectacular combination. Others have bright blue and orange patterns.

Gobies are very interesting fishes and very hardy, a combination that should make them very popular aquarium fishes. Like blennies, however, they have not captured the attention of the aquarist, except of course for a few extraordinary species.

It would normally not be expected that gobies, because of their small size, form a source of food for human consumption. But in the Philippines the *Ipon* (Ilocano) fisheries are still capturing millions of these fishes for market. Actually ipon are the fry of several species of gobies. They are captured at the mouths of rivers as they return to the areas from which their parents came. The mature gobies head downstream and into the sea to spawn. The returning fry are captured by the millions, many of which are converted into a sort of fish sauerkraut or fish silage called Bagoong.

302. *Gobiodon quinquestrigatus* (Cuvier & Valenciennes). Adult. Philippine Islands. Five-lined goby. Photo by U. Erich Friese.

303. *Tridentiger trigonocephalus* (Gill). 40 mm standard length. Aburatsubo, Kanagawa, Japan. Striped goby.

304. *Eviota abax* (Jordan & Snyder). 30 mm standard length. Shimoda, Shizuoka, Japan. Skipper.

305. *Bathygobius fuscus* (Rüppell). 30 mm standard length. Shimoda, Shizuoka, Japan. Dusky goby.

306. *Eleotroides elapoides* (Günther). 40 mm standard length. Aburatsubo, Kanagawa, Japan. Stretched silk goby.

307. *Nemaptereleotis magnificus* 35 mm standard length. Pescadores Islands, Taiwan. Firefish.

308. *Nemaptereleotis magnificus* Fowler. 58 mm standard length. Moorea, Society Islands. Photo by Dr. John E. Randall.

309. *Periophthalmus cantonensis* (Osbeck). 30 mm standard length. Indo-Pacific. Chinese mud-skipper.

310. *Periophthalmus papilio* (Bloch & Schneider). Adult. The butterfly-mudskipper is able to move about on muddy shores and rocks quite rapidly. Collecting these fishes is a difficult procedure for the inexperienced collector.

311. *Acentrogobius hoshinonis* (Tanaka). 50 mm standard length. Aburatsubo, Kanagawa, Japan. Blue-spotted goby.

312. *Chasmichthys dolichognathus* (Hilgendorf). 30 mm standard length. Aburatsubo, Kanagawa, Japan. Snakeskin goby.

313. *Sagamia genionema* (Hilgendorf). 40 mm standard length. Aburatsubo, Kanagawa, Japan. Bearded goby.

314. *Chasmichthys gulosus* (Guichenot). 50 mm standard length. Aburatsubo, Kanagawa, Japan. Thicklipped goby.

315. Unidentified goby, possibly *Zonogonius boreus* swimming upside down. About 25 mm standard length. Okinawa.

316. *Acanthogobius flavi-manus* (Temminck & Schlegel). 100 mm standard length. Aburatsubo, Kanagawa, Japan. Yellowfin goby.

317. *Pterogobius zonoleucus* Jordan & Snyder. 40 mm standard length. Moroiso, Kanagawa, Japan. Silky goby. This species should not be confused with the one in fig. 306.

318. *Pogonoculius zebra* Fowler. 25 mm standard length. Amami-Oshima Island. Zebra goby.

179

319. *Amphiprion clarkii*
(Bennett). 50 mm
standard length.
Aburatsubo Marine
Park, Japan. The
yellow-tailed
anemonefish in its
dark phase.
Previously this fish
was known under the
scientific name
*Amphiprion
xanthurus.*

320. *Amphiprion clarkii*
(Bennett). 30 mm
standard length.
Okinawa. The
juvenile color
pattern of the yellow-
tailed anemonefish is
slightly different (see
adult, figs. 319 and
321).

Family POMACENTRIDAE

DAMSELFISHES AND ANEMONEFISHES

Within the family Pomacentridae there is a group of species that have evolved a behavior pattern which is unusual. These fishes, the anemonefishes, live within the tentacles of sea anemones. Other fishes coming into contact with these tentacles will trigger the stinging cells or nematocysts of the anemones and possibly even be killed by them. The anemonefishes apparently have evolved a mechanism which inhibits the triggering of the nematocysts. They swim about the dangerous tentacles with apparent immunity. It has been said that they lure unsuspecting predators into the anemone, the predator being killed and eaten by it. This would be a fair trade: the fish gets protection, the anemone gets food. The immunity of the anemonefishes apparently is involved with the mucous coating of its body, for if the mucus is removed the fish is stung like any other fish.

Normally the anemonefishes swim above the sea anemones, eating the small zooplankters that are carried past by the currents. When they are disturbed they dart into the tentacles for protection. They will nervously peer out of the tentacles at intervals to see if the danger is gone.

Usually only one species of anemonefish will inhabit a particular anemone. Other species of fishes may share the anemone, but not other anemonefishes. The type of anemone selected is also relatively specific. In captivity the fishes are less selective in their choice of anemones; Pacific fishes, for example, have been known to accept Caribbean anemones. Normally, only two fishes, a male and a female, will inhabit an anemone, spawning close by and using the anemone as a deterrent to other fishes that might want to eat the eggs.

Damselfishes are small reef fishes, usually brightly colored, with only two anal spines. They have small mouths provided with conical or incisiform teeth, the number of rows and types being important in distinguishing the genera.

Pomacentrids comprise a large family of fishes with variable food habits. Some, as mentioned above, are plankton feeders, whereas others are strictly herbivores. Still others feed on small invertebrate animals that can be found on the reef. Most damselfishes are omnivores, eating both plant and animal material.

Most damselfishes spawn alike. The male clears off a section of a rock and sets up a strongly defended territory. Pomacentrids in general are territorial fishes, but during the breeding season the defense of the territory becomes much more aggressive. There may be a color change in the male. The male signals to passing females that he is ready to spawn by making looping motions above the nest. A female with eggs may accept the invitation and is led to the proper site where she is to deposit the eggs. Upon completion of egg deposition, the female is chased from the nest and the looping signals begin once again. Once several females have spawned with the male, he sets up a guard over the eggs until they hatch. All potentially dangerous animals are chased, including fishes much larger than itself and even humans. The male will use its fins to fan the egg, providing an oxygenating current over them. When the eggs hatch the male's job is over, and the young damselfishes must fend for themselves. The eggs are oval and are always attached to the substrate.

Many damselfishes use the reef for protection, darting among coral branches when danger threatens. Species of the genus *Dascyllus* probably form the intermediate stage between the anemonefishes and the rest of the damselfishes. They usually hide among the coral branches but can also become adapted to living with the sea anemones like the anemonefishes of the *Amphiprion*.

The eggs of this anemonefish species have been laid well within the protective shadow of the host anemone; the fish shown is the male parent *Amphiprion perideraion*. Photo by Dr. Gerald R. Allen.

321. *Amphiprion clarkii* (Bennett). 30 mm standard length. Okinawa. The white bands in this species extend along the upper edges of the fins.

322. *Amphiprion polymnus* (Linnaeus). 20 mm standard length. Okinawa. The juvenile saddle-back clownfish ıs similar to the adult seen below (fig. 323).

323. *Amphiprion polymnus* (Linnaeus). 60 mm standard length. The saddle-back clownfish was previously known under the name *Amphiprion laticlavius.*

324. *Amphiprion frenatus* Brevoort. 30 mm standard length. Okinawa. Red clownfish.

325. *Amphiprion frenatus* Brevoort. 30 mm standard length. Okinawa. Red clownfish juvenile.

326. *Amphiprion clarkii* (Bennett). 50 mm standard length. Okinawa. Yellow-tailed anemonefish.

327. *Amphiprion perideraion* Bleeker. 30 mm standard length. Okinawa. Skunk clownfish.

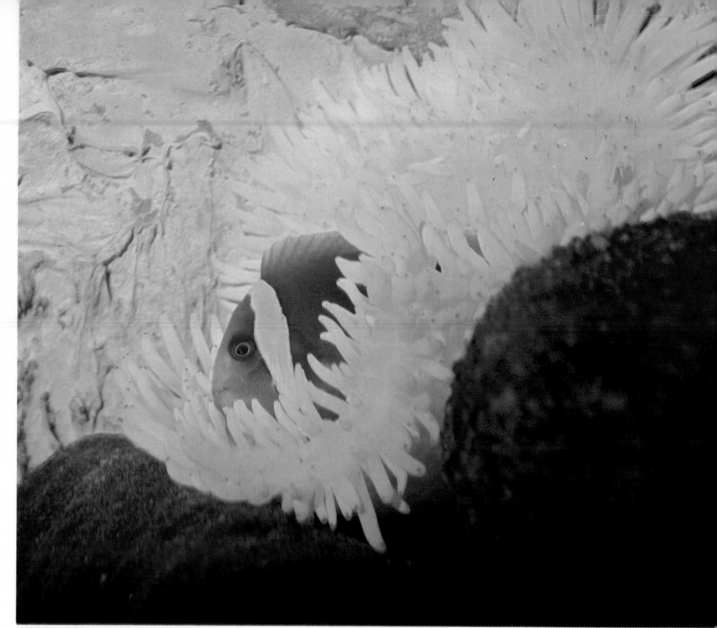

328. *Amphiprion frenatus*
Brevoort. 50 mm standard
length. Aburatsubo Marine Park,
Japan. Red clownfish.

329. *Amphiprion
frenatus*
Brevoort. 50 mm
standard length.
Okinawa. The
red clownfish
will not often be
separated from
the protective
tentacles of its
host anemone
and will appear
more often as in
figure 328.

186

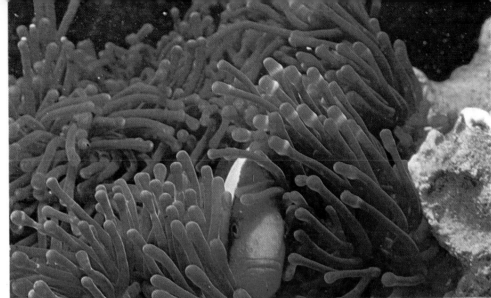

330. *Amphiprion
frenatus* Brevoort.
50 mm standard
length. Okinawa.
Red clownfish.

331. *Amphiprion
frenatus* Brevoort.
50 mm standard
length. Okinawa.
Red clownfish.

332. *Amphiprion
frenatus* Brevoort.
30 mm standard
length. Okinawa.
Red clownfish.

333. *Amphiprion ocellaris* Cuvier. 40 mm standard length. Okinawa. Clown anemonefish.

334. *Amphiprion percula* (Lacépède). About 40 mm standard length. Clownfish.

335. *Amphiprion sandaracinos* Allen. 30 mm standard length. Okinawa. Skunk clownfish.

336. *Amphiprion ocellaris* Cuvier. The lighter color differentiates this species from *Amphiprion percula* (fig. 334).

337. *Amphiprion
biaculeatus*
(Bloch). 30 mm
Philippine Islands.
Spine-cheeked
anemonefish.

338. *Abudefduf
cyaneus* (Quoy
& Gaimard). 30
mm. Okinawa.
Blue reef-fish.

339. *Chromis atripectoralis*
Schultz & Welander.
Okinawa. Blue
chromis.

340. *Amphiprion chrysopterus* Cuvier. 123 mm standard length. Bora Bora, Society Islands. The female orange-finned anemonefish has taken up residence in the anemone, *Radianthus paumotensis*. Photo by Dr. Gerald R. Allen.

341. *Abudefduf cyaneus* swimming about the branches of the stagshorn coral *Acropora.*

342. *Abudefduf bengalensis* (Bloch). 25 mm standard length. Shimoda, Shizuoka, Japan. Bengal devil.

343. *Abudefduf sordidus* (Forskål). 30 mm standard length. Shimoda, Shizuoka, Japan. Kupipi (Hawaiian name).

344. *Abudefduf sexfasciatus* (Lacépède). 30 mm standard length. Shimoda, Shizuoka, Japan. Chinese sergeant-major.

345. *Abudefduf saxatilis (Linnaeus)*. 30 mm standard length. Shimoda, Shizuoka, Japan. Sergeant-major.

346. *Abudefduf thoracotaeniatus* Fowler & Bean. 40 mm standard length. Philippine Islands. Bar-chested damselfish.

347. *Chromis analis* (Cuvier). 30 mm standard length. Izu Marine Park, Japan. Yellow devil.

348. Unidentified damselfish, about 40 mm standard length, from the Izu Marine Park, Japan.

349. *Pomacentrus coelestis* Jordan & Starks. 46 mm standard length. Eniwetok, Marshall Islands. Photo by Dr. John E. Randall.

350. *Abudefduf cyaneus* (Quoy & Gaimard). Adults. Taipei Aquarium, Taipei. Blue reef fish. Photo by K. H. Choo.

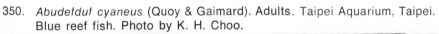

*Dascyllus
marginatus*
About 80 mm
standard length.

Photo by Dr. Herbert R. Axelrod.

351. *Abudefduf leucogaster.* 87 mm standard length. Palau Islands. Photo by Dr. John E. Randall.

352. *Abudefduf behnii* (Bleeker). About 45 mm standard length. Philippine Islands. Photo by Earl Kennedy.

353. *Pomacentrus dorsalis.* 30 mm standard length. Okinawa.

354. *Pomacentrus amboinensis* Bleeker. 30 mm standard length. Okinawa. The two black spots, one at the upper edge of the opercle and the other at the upper edge of the pectoral fin base, are the clues to the identity of this species.

355. *Abudefduf johnstanianus.* 40 mm standard length. Okinawa. Blackbar devil.

356. *Dascyllus aruanus* (Linnaeus). 30 mm standard length. Okinawa. White-tailed damselfish.

357. *Abudefduf rex* (Snyder). 30 mm standard length. Okinawa. King damselfish.

358. Aberrant color phase of *Abudefduf cyaneus* (Fowler). 20 mm standard length. Yellow-tailed blue devil.

359. *Abudefduf melanopus* (Bleeker). 30 mm standard length. Okinawa. Yellow-backed damselfish.

360. *Pomacentrus coelestis* Jordan & Starks. 20 mm standard length. Aburatsubo, Kanagawa, Japan. An older individual of this species is shown in figure 349.

361. *Abudefduf biocellatus* (Quoy & Gaimard). 20 mm standard length. Ibusuki, Kagoshima, Japan. Twinspot damselfish.

362. *Dascyllus melanurus* Bleeker. 30 mm standard length. Philippine Islands. Black-tailed damselfish.

363. *Dascyllus trimaculatus* (Rüppell). About 20 mm standard length. Koajiro, Kanagawa, Japan. Three-spot damselfish.

364. *Dascyllus reticulatus* (Richardson). 20 mm standard length. Okinawa. Reticulated damselfish.

365. *Abudefduf behnii*
(Bleeker). 30 mm
standard length.
Okinawa. It is
surprising that
this attractive
fish escaped
discovery until
1929.

366. *Abudefduf
cyaneus* . 30 mm
standard length.
Ishigaki Island.
Although similar
to *P. coelestis*
(fig. 349) this
fish seems to be
a different
species.

367. *Abudefduf
oxyodon*
(Bleeker). 30
mm standard
length.
Philippine
Islands. Blue-
streak devil.

368. *Abudefduf lacrymatus* (Quoy & Gaimard). 20 mm standard length. Okinawa.

369. *Chromis dimidiatus* (Klunzinger). 30 mm standard length. Okinawa. This bicolored condition appears in other species of damselfish, including one from the Caribbean.

370. *Chromis notatus* (Temminck & Schlegel). 40 mm standard length. Moroiso, Kanagawa Japan. Tail-light damselfish.

Family SYNGNATHIDAE

SEA HORSES AND PIPEFISHES

The outstanding characteristic of the fishes of this family is that their bodies are encased in a sort of armor composed of modified scales. These scales are arranged in rings, the number of which help determine the identity of the species. Syngnathids can easily be divided into two major groups, the sea horses and the pipefishes.

The sea horses differ from the pipefishes and from most other fishes for that matter, in having their heads set at an angle to the body. This characteristic and the shape of the head have combined to produce the effect that earned them their common name, sea horses. The tail is prehensile and is used to anchor the fishes to a blade of grass, a sea whip, or other bottom features.

Sea horses depend upon warm currents to bring small planktonic animals to them. Their means of locomotion is a small dorsal fin in the middle of the back and two pectoral fins just behind the head. Most of the time they remain in one spot and let the current do the work.

One of the most amazing characteristics of the sea horses and pipefishes is that the male incubates the eggs and gives birth to the living young. There is a ritualized spawning sequence in which the fishes are intertwined with one another, the eggs being deposited in a specialized brood pouch or attached directly to the abdomen or even the tail of the male. The eggs develop for some eight to ten days and eventually hatch, at which time they are forcibly expelled by contortions of the male or, when not in the pouch, are released directly. The young are tiny replicas of the parents; even the tiniest of young sea horses can use their tails to avoid being swept away by the current.

There are between 25 and 30 species of sea horses but more than 150 species of pipefishes. Unlike the sea horses they have a tail fin. The presence of this fin, coupled with the lack of angulation of the head, makes it easy to distinguish the pipefishes from the sea horses.

Most sea horses are found in grass beds or floating sea-weed of some kind, but pipefishes have a greater variety of habitats. Although their main habitat is the grass beds, they can be found in coral reefs as well; some species can even be found in fresh water.

The pipefishes are usually six to eight inches in length, although the largest gets to be some 18 inches in length. Some pipefishes are extremely colorful, having electric blue lines or banded patterns of yellow and black. Most, however, are shades of green or brown, colors which easily blend into a grass bed type habitat.

Pipefishes are slow-swimming fishes that feed on small invertebrate animals or larval fishes. The long, tube-like snout is used to suck in these animals with extraordinary accuracy and swiftness. The dorsal and caudal fins provide the main means of locomotion.

Specific recognition of the pipefishes depends on the position of the fins in reference to the rings, the number of rings for the different sections of the body, and the number, extent, and position of various ridges on the body.

The eyes of the sea horses and pipefishes move independently. It is interesting to watch the two eyes, since one may be watching you while the one on the other side of the head is taking in the scenery elsewhere.

Although sea horses are quite popular in home aquaria, pipefishes rarely are kept. Sea horses have also been used as a major design pattern when decorating something with a marine motif. Along with the starfish, the sea horse probably is among the most widely known of all sea animals for this reason. It may also be because sea horses have been known to man for an extremely long time; they were described by Pliny the Elder, who lived around 50 A.D.

371. *Hippocampus kuda* (Bleeker). Indo-Pacific, including the Hawaiian Islands. Photo by G. Marcuse.

Hippocampus mohnikei (Temminck & Schlegel). 40 mm standard length. Shimoda, Shizuoka, Japan.

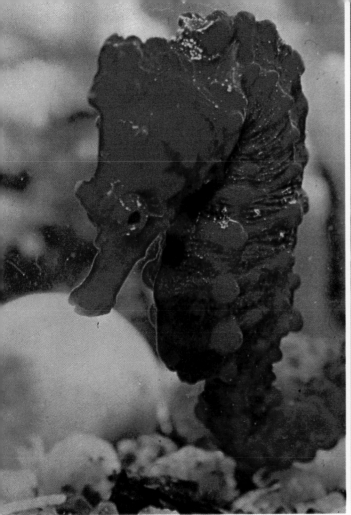

373. *Hippocampus japonicus* Kaup. 30 mm standard length. Shimoda, Shizuoka, Japan. Japanese sea horse.

374. *Hippocampus coronatus* (Temminck & Schlegel). 40 mm standard length. Moroiso, Kanagawa, Japan. Crowned sea horse.

375. *Hippocampus kuda* Bleeker. Indo-Pacific region. Oceanic sea horse. Photo by H. Hansen.

376. *Hippocampus coronatus*
(Temminck & Schlegel).
40 mm standard length.
Moroiso, Kanagawa, Japan.
The main propulsion of the
sea horse is the small
fin on its back. Needless
to say the sea horse is a
very poor swimmer. Its
prehensile tail keeps it
anchored while water
currents bring food to it.

377. *Hippocampus coronatus*
(Temminck & Schlegel).
40 mm standard length.
This *male* crowned sea
horse is giving birth to tiny
replicas of itself. The eggs
are deposited in its pouch
during the spawning
process and the male takes
over the chores of
incubation and birth.

378. An unidentified pipefish, about 80 mm standard length, from Izu Marine Park, Japan.

379. *Doryrhamphus melanopleura* (Bleeker): 50 mm standard length. Ibusuki, Kagoshima, Japan.

Family SOLENOSTOMIDAE
GHOST PIPEFISHES

Ghost pipefishes, as can be seen by the accompanying photographs, are close relatives of the sea horses and pipefishes. The head greatly resembles that of the pipefishes but the body is quite different. The body is expanded behind the head to accommodate the first dorsal fin and the pelive fins. The body is also expanded posteriorly where the second dorsal fin and anal fin are positioned. The body in between is as slender as the head. The tail is very long.

There are about five species known in this family, and all can be placed in the single genus *Solenostomus*.

Contrary to the breeding habits of the sea horses and pipefishes, the female ghost pipefishes have the brood pouches and care for the young. The pouch of a female ghost pipefish is formed by the pelvic fins, whose inner margins are attached to the abdomen. The eggs are kept in this pouch area by means of short filaments. In the males, as might be expected, the pelvic fins are not attached to the body.

Ghost pipefishes are usually found among the sea-weeds. Their shape and coloration make them very difficult to see.

Very little is known about these small, uncommon fishes.

Hippocampus
sp. 132 mm standard length.
Adult. (No collection data available).

380. *Solenichthys* sp. Adult. Great Barrier Reef, Australia. Photo by Lloyd Grigg.

381. *Solenostomus paegnius* Jordan & Thompson. 80 mm standard length. Izu Marine Park, Japan. Ghost pipefish.

382. *Solenostomus paegnius* Jordan & Thompson. About 80 mm standard length. Izu Marine Park, Japan. The blotchy color may be the result of a disease that commonly affects sea horses and pipefishes.

383. *Solenostomus paegnius* Jordan & Thompson. About 80 mm standard length. Izu Marine Park. Although the color is quite different this is the same species as represented in figure 381.

384. *Solenostomus paegnius* Jordan & Thompson. About 80 mm standard length. Izu Marine Park, Japan. Ghost pipefish.

385. *Synchiropus* sp. (possibly *S. ocellatus*). 30 mm standard length. Izu Marine Park, Japan.

386. *Pegasus volitans* Linnaeus. 30 mm standard length. Ito Aquarium, Japan. Dragon fish.

Family CALLIONYMIDAE

DRAGONETS

The fishes of the family Callionymidae are very interesting to both the aquarist and the scientist. The current scientific literature about those fishes is incomplete and most confusing. To add to the complexity of the problem, there may be extreme cases of sexual dimorphism, where the shape of the body and fins of the male may be quite different from that of the female. Sexual dichromatism is also widespread throughout this group.

Because these fishes are so difficult to capture without the use of traps or poisons, the collections of these species are fairly scanty. As an example, when the authors tried to identify the species known as the psychedelic fish, *Synchiropus picturatus*, we were able to locate only a single specimen, (the original type of Peters) in Berlin, and the specimen was a mere one inch long! Of course, additional specimens have since been added to the United States National Museum in Washington (specifically, those which appear in the photographs!).

The genera composing the family Callionymidae are basically categorized by having either a single dorsal fin or two dorsals. Only the genus *Draculo* has a single dorsal. The two-dorsal genera are *Diplogrammus, Amora, Eleutherochir, Paracallionymus, Yerutius, Callionymus, Synchiropus,* and *Dactylopus.*

Until the spring of 1972, few if any

387. *Synchiropus splendidus* (Herre). Adult. Philippine Islands. Mandarin fish. Photo by Dr. Herbert R. Axelrod.

388. *Synchiropus picturatus* (Peters). Adult. Philippine Islands. Psychedelic fish. Photo by Dr. Herbert R. Axelrod.

living specimens of *Synchiropus* were ever exhibited in an aquarium. Though originally labelled *Callionymus splendidus* by Herre and *C. picturatus* by Peters, both fishes have been referred to the genus *Synchiropus*. With the availability of additional material and the high value which aquarists have placed on the fish, it won't be long before collections of additional species will make their appearance.

As is true of many species in which males are very different from the females, the two species *S. splendidus* and *S. picturatus* exhibit extremes of territorialism, and a definite 'pecking order' becomes established when more than one male is maintained in a large aquarium. There are frequent examples of combat between competing males, and death usually results from such combat for the loser. These two species spend most of their time resting on the bottom of the aquarium; they relish live *Tubifex* worms as well as some frozen and freeze-dried brine shrimp. They would probably do best if maintained separately without other members of the family with them.

According to the scientific descriptions of several of the members of the other genera, none seem comparable to *S. splendidus* or *S. picturatus* in terms of color pattern or gaudiness.

Family LUTJANIDAE
SNAPPERS

The snappers are difficult fishes to characterize, being generalized perch-like fishes like the groupers and grunts. The shape of the snout and the enlarged canines at the tip of the jaws give them a distinctive appearance that most people who are familiar with fishes can easily recognize. Technically they have a maxillary for the most part slipping under the edge of the suborbital bone and thus hidden from view when the mouth is closed; teeth on the roof of the mouth; and no spines on the edge of the gill cover as found in the groupers.

The sharp teeth are used for grasping prey, which may be fishes or crustaceans. Snappers are found on reefs during the day, sometimes in large schools, and over the grass flats at night foraging for food.

Snappers are food fishes and are actively sought by various fisheries. Unfortunately, some of the snappers are responsible for ciguatera poisoning. The poisonous nature, however, seems to depend upon the time of the year and the geographic area in which the snappers are caught. It may be of interest to note here that although the snappers are very widespread in the Pacific Ocean there are very few in the Hawaiian Islands. Some of the Hawaiian snappers were introduced artificially.

Most of the snappers are inshore fishes inhabiting the shallow waters of the coasts. There are some deeper-water forms.

Estimates of the number of snappers appear to settle between 250 to 300 different species. They are moderate-sized, reaching lengths of two to three feet, although reports from skin divers place the maximum size at about twice this size.

Most of the species of snappers are included in the genus *Lutjanus*. Another genus, *Caesio*, has a more elongate body, and its single dorsal fin has slender spines. They are less tied to the bottom than the other species and are often seen in very large schools around the reef. The species of the genus *Caesio* are usually called fusiliers. They migrate long distances in their search for food. The bright iridescent colors of these fishes make a school of them a sight to behold.

Snappers produce large numbers of pelagic eggs. The initial development of the larval snappers occurs in these oceanic waters. They return to shore after about six weeks and undergo a color metamorphosis into the juvenile forms. Larval snappers as far as known do not exhibit any specialized structures for flotation or defense.

Among one of the more colorful snappers is the emperor snapper, *Lutjanus sebae*. The red and white banded pattern is present in juveniles but is lost with age, the adult being a plain reddish fish.

Another brightly colored snapper is the blue-striped snapper, *Lutjanus kasmira*. It is a common snapper of the Indo-Pacific region, often found in schools of several hundred individuals. The yellow and blue coloration creates a spectacular sight. They feed upon the usual snapper diet of fish and crustaceans.

One of the snappers, *Lutjanus nematophorus,* has the anterior dorsal fin rays extended into long filaments, giving the fin a rather un-snapperlike appearance. They gradually become reduced in size; by the time the fish reach maturity (at about two feet or more) the fin is normal.

The nemipterids sometimes are classified as a subfamily of the snappers, sometimes as a family by themselves. They lack the teeth on the roof of the mouth of the true snappers.

The two-lined snapper, *Scolopsis bilineatus,* belongs to the nemipterids. It is sometimes called a spine-cheeked snapper because of the presence of a strong spine below the eye. It is a coral reef fish.

Family POMADASYIDAE

GRUNTS.

Grunts are difficult to tell apart from the snappers. The head profile is different as well as the dentition. The teeth are never developed as prominent canines like those of the snappers. In addition the grunts have strong pharyngeal teeth.

These fishes grind their pharyngeal teeth together, producing the characteristic grunting noises. These noises are amplified by the swim bladder and can be picked up by hydrophones. When a grunt is removed from the water, the grunting noise it makes is quite audible.

Grunts are panfish but are not as sought after for food as the snappers or groupers.

Large numbers of grunts can be seen milling around the reefs by day, sometimes every fish being oriented in the same direction, probably facing the current. At night they scatter over the grass flats to forage for food. Their diet consists mainly of small bottom invertebrates.

A strange behavioral trait of the grunts has been observed. Two grunts will orient themselves face to face with their mouths open to the extreme; they then press their mouths together. Whether this is a test of strength before mating or a fighting posture in defense of a territory is not known.

Usually included in the grunts, though sometimes given their own family, are the sweetlips, or gaterins. The gaterins are difficult to identify because of their capacity to undergo changes from juvenile to adult. Juveniles are usually colorful, with striking patterns; adults are more somber-colored and with less spectacular patterns.

The young sweetlips have a peculiar swimming motion, more like a fluttering movement than purposeful swimming. This characteristic swimming disappears when the fish changes color. It has been reported that the young gaterins live in some sort of association with fishes of the family Centriscidae (snipe-fishes).

The sweetlips usually have thick lips and a row of six pores just posterior to the lower lip. The largest genus of the sweetlips is the genus *Gaterin.*

Family THERAPONIDAE

TIGERFISHES

The tigerfishes are small- to moderate-size fishes inhabiting fresh, brackish, or salt water. They are conspicuously striped, the markings continued onto the tail fin. The freshwater tigerfishes are valuable as food fishes, but the marine species are not.

Therapon jarbua, the three-striped tigerfish, is the best known of these fishes and often finds its way into the home marine aquarium. They usually do well in an aquarium if not frightened unduly. They are susceptible to shock.

Young tigerfishes appear to be territorial in behavior. They select a small area for themselves and defend it against other tigerfishes of roughly the same size. With age, however, this territoriality is generally lost.

Therapon theraps, the Australian common name for which is the grunter, is wide-ranging as well as completely adaptable to various salinities of water. It undergoes a color transformation from juvenile to adult. Young fishes have five bands surrounding the body, but as the fish ages the bands break up into spots and become rearranged as four longitudinal lines.

Like the groupers, the tigerfishes have sharp spines on the opercle.

389. *Scolopsis bilineatus* (Bloch). 130 mm standard length. Okinawa. Two-lined snapper.

390. *Caesio chrysozonus* Cuvier & Valenciennes. 60 mm standard length. Okinawa. Yellow-striped caesio.

391. *Gaterin diagrammus* (Linnaeus). 60 mm standard length. Okinawa. Diagram sweetlips.

392. *Spilotichthys pictus* (Thunberg). 180 mm standard length. Okinawa. Painted sweetlips.

393. *Spilotichthys pictus* (Thunberg). 60 mm standard length. Kamakura, Kanagawa, Japan. Juvenile.

394. *Gaterin chaetodonoides* (Lacépède). 150 mm standard length. Aburatsubo Marine Park, Japan. Clown sweetlips.

395. *Lutjanus* sp. 40 mm standard length. Shimoda, Shizuoka, Japan. Yellow-striped snapper.

396. *Lutjanus chrysotaenia* (Bleeker) and *Lutjanus kasmira* (Forskål) (background).

397. *Lutjanus fulviflamma* (Forskål) Underwater photograph of an individual estimated to be about 130 mm standard length. Ogasawara Islands, Japan.

398. *Symphorichthys spilurus* (Günther). 180 mm standard length. Philippine Islands. Blue-and-gold striped snapper.

399. *Lutjanus kasmira* (Forskål). 60 mm standard length. Okinawa. The adult of this species is in the background of figure 396.

400. *Symphorus nematophorus* (Bleeker). 130 mm standard length. Philippine Islands. Blue-lined snapper.

401. *Macolor niger* (Forskål). 30 mm standard length. Moroiso, Kanagawa, Japan. This black-and-white snapper is often confused with members of the genus *Gaterin*.

402. *Gaterin chaetodonoides* (Lacépède). 60 mm standard length. Okinawa. The adult of this species is depicted in figure 394.

403. *Therapon oxyrhinchus* (Temminck & Schlegel). 150 mm standard length. Enoshima, Japan.

404. *Ostichthys japonicus* (Cuvier & Valenciennes). 160 mm standard length. Okinawa. Japanese soldierfish.

405. *Therapon theraps* Cuvier & Valenciennes. Ueno Zoo Aquarium, Japan. Striped grunter.

Family HOLOCENTRIDAE

SQUIRREL FISHES

The squirrelfishes are reef fishes with a predominantly red color. There are additional markings of white, yellow, or black, the pattern of the dorsal fin being important in distinguishing the species.

Along with the red coloration, squirrelfishes have large eyes typical of fishes which are nocturnal. During the day squirrelfishes hide in caves or other dark places, and it is only at night that they venture out onto the reef to hunt for food.

Squirrelfishes are very spiny fishes, rough to the touch because of the strongly ctenoid scales, and with the head armed with several spines. In some genera (*Adioryx, Flammeo,* and *Holocentrus*) there is a long sharp spine on the preopercular bone. In some species this spine may cause painful wounds, possibly because of the presence of a toxic substance.

The seventy or more species of squirrelfishes are all from the tropical areas of the world, mostly around coral reefs. They usually remain in a specific area, not moving about like some of the migratory fishes.

Squirrelfishes lay pelagic eggs, the early development taking place in the open waters away from the reef. The larvae are highly modified, very spiny creatures so different from the adults that they were given a new name, *Rhinchichthys,* with the idea that they represented a different type of fish entirely. The name is still used as a general term for the larvae. Prominent in the *rhinchichthys* larvae is an extended rostrum, almost like that of a billfish. The spiny covering does not prevent the larvae from being eaten by large fishes, as squirrelfish larvae have been found in the stomachs of tunas and dolphins.

Squirrelfishes have been known to produce sounds. These sounds are probably emitted during courtship and/or during aggressive encounters. Dr. Earl Herald of the Steinhart Aquarium, San Francisco, told of hearing sounds made by a group of squirrelfishes kept in a display tank. The squirrelfishes were *Adioryx xantherythrus,* from the Hawaiian Islands. Dr. Herald observed that the individuals that were making the sounds assumed a position in which the tails were close together and the anterior parts of their bodies were separated. This he considered to be courting behavior.

Squirrelfishes are used for food in many areas. In Hawaii several squirrelfishes are eaten, but the most prized species is *Myripristis murdjan* or, as it is called in the Islands, menpachi. The name menpachi is now generally used for all species of the genus *Myripristis* in the Hawaiian Islands.

Myripristis, as well as the genera *Ostichthys, Corniger,* and *Plectrypops,* belongs to the subfamily of squirrelfishes that do not have the strong spine on the corner of the preopercular bone. One of the species, *Ostichthys japonicus,* is reported to be the deepest-living squirrelfish. This group of squirrelfishes is more likely to be found in groups or small schools rather than individually or in pairs, as in the other group (*Adioryx, Holocentrus,* and *Flammeo*).

The food of squirrelfishes consists mainly of crustaceans (crabs, shrimp, etc.). These they usually hunt at night. As mentioned before, the squirrelfishes have large eyes, usually a necessity for a nocturnal existence. When kept in captivity the squirrelfishes should be provided with areas in which they can be protected from the bright lights. Their sensitive eyes would be damaged if too much exposure to light is forced upon them.

The red color is another characteristic common to nocturnal animals. At night the red color is very difficult to see against the inky black background of the water. In deep-water fishes similar adaptations are found, i.e., large eyes and red color patterns. The first is due to the low light levels common to both evening and deep water. The second adaptation is probably tied up with the loss of the red end of the spectrum very quickly with depth. Any red creature appears gray below 30 or 40 feet. The contrasting whites and yellows often seen on squirrelfishes tend to offset the "protective" red coloration and may be a sort of species recognition pattern or warning signal. The dorsal fin is fluttered up and down rapidly, making the dorsal fin pattern very conspicuous and therefore of much importance.

The names used here, *Adioryx* and *Flammeo,* are generally relegated to the status of subgenera. However, recent studies on the squirrelfishes have pointed out that they deserve full generic rank. Although they are not fully accepted by every ichthyologist, their usage is becoming more and more common.

Fishes of another family, the Priacanthidae, are similar in appearance to the squirrelfishes in having the red coloration and large eyes. The priacanthids, or bigeyes as they are commonly called, are not closely related to the squirrelfishes in spite of this resemblance. Their habits are similar, however, as the priacanthids too are nocturnal fishes, and their prime food is crustaceans, although fishes and worms are also prominent items in their diet.

The dorsal fin of the bigeyes is continuous, whereas that of the squirrelfishes is deeply incised, almost forming two separate fins. The anal fin of the bigeyes is also much longer and lacks the enlargement of the middle anal fin spine that the squirrelfishes possess.

The bigeyes are usually found in deeper water than the squirrelfishes, and grow to a larger size, up to two feet. Like the squirrelfishes, they are sometimes used for food. In Hawaii *Priacanthus cruentatus* comes into shallow water and is often taken by spear by skin divers.

406. *Myripristis* sp. 132 mm standard length. Eniwetok, Marshall Islands. Photo by Dr. John E. Randall.

407. *Myripristis murdjan* (Forskål). 120 mm standard length. Aburatsubo Marine Park, Japan. Bigeye squirrelfish.

408. *Gnathodentex   aurolineatum* (Lacépède). 130 mm standard   length.   Ogasa wara Island, Japan.

409. *Myripristis kuntee* (Cuvier & Valenciennes). 120 mm standard length. Okinawa. Blacktip soldierfish.

410. *Flammeo sammara* (Forskål). 80 mm standard length. Ueno Zoo Aquarium. Big-spine squirrelfish.

411. *Adioryx diadema* (Lacépède). 100 mm. Okinawa. Barred squirrelfish.

412. *Adioryx spinifer* (Forskål). 160 mm standard length. Okinawa. One of the largest of the squirrelfishes, the long-jawed squirrelfish grows to about 18 inches in length.

413. *Adioryx ruber* (Forskål). 120 mm standard length. Okinawa. African squirrelfish.

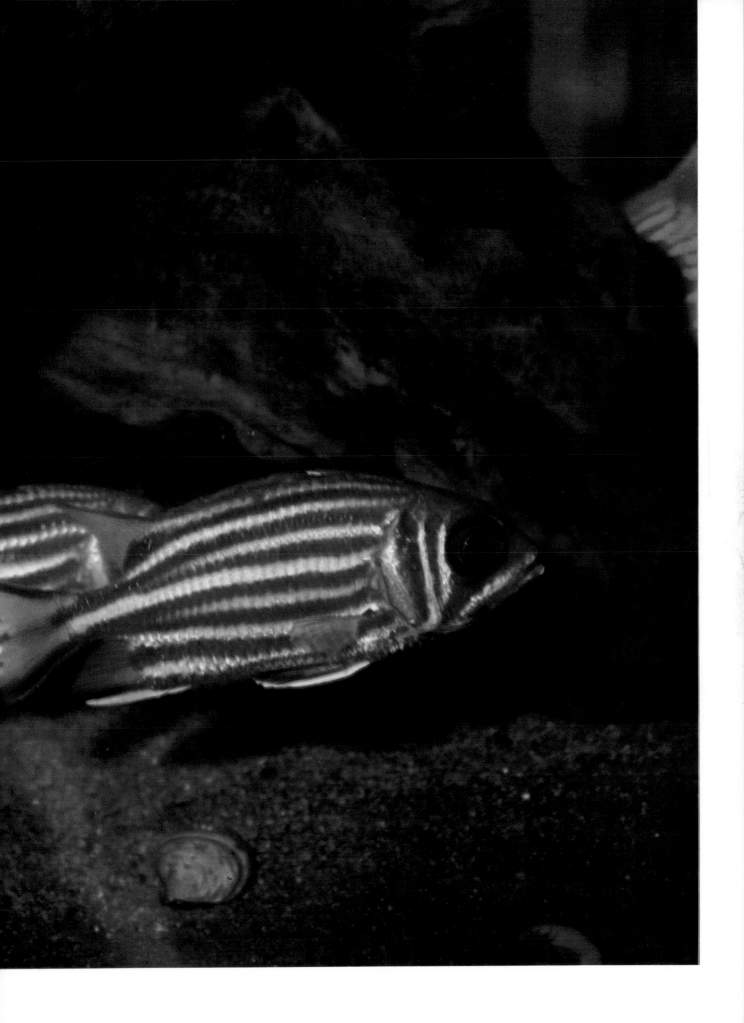

414. *Kuhlia taeniura* (Cuvier & Valenciennes). 180 mm standard length. Okinawa. Reef trout or aholehole (Hawaiian name).

415. *Leiognathus nuchilis* (Temminck & Schlegel). 40 mm standard length. Aburatsubo, Kanagawa, Japan. Slimy; soapy.

417. *Remora* sp. 180 mm standard length. Bismarck Sea.

416. *Sillago sihama* (Forskål). About 200 mm standard length. Aburatsubo, Kanagawa, Japan. Sandsmelt.

418. *Kyphosus cinerascens* (Forskål). 40 mm standard length. Kamakura, Kanagawa. Juveniles of this chub are often found in floating seaweeds as *Sargassum*.

419. *Mylio macrocephalus* (Basilewsky). 40 mm standard length. Kanagawa. Juvenile Black porgy.

420. *Hapalogenys nigripinnis* (Temminck & Schlegel). 300 mm standard length. Aburatsubo Marine Park, Japan.

421. *Sacura margaritacea* (Hilgendorf). 130 mm standard length. Izu Marine Park, Japan. Adult male.

422. *Sacura margaritacea* (Hilgendorf). 100 mm standard length. Aburatsubo Marine Park, Japan. Adult female.

423. *Pseudanthias taira* Schmidt. 60 mm standard length. Miyako Island, Japan.

424. *Franzia fasciatus* Kamohara. 80 mm standard length. Izu Marine Park, Japan.

425. *Paramia quinquelineata* (Cuvier & Valenciennes). 60 mm standard length. Ito, Shizuoka, Japan. Five-lined cardinalfish.

426. *Apogon semilineatus* (Temminck & Schlegel). 80 mm standard length. Moroiso, Kanagawa, Japan. Indian little fish.

427. One of the schooling species of cardinalfishes. They will usually remain close to shelter, such as these coral formations, and disappear into them whenever danger threatens.

Family APOGONIDAE

CARDINALFISHES

Cardinalfishes are small fishes, usually about four inches in length, rarely exceeding twice that size. Estimates as to the number of species included in this family range from a low of 75 to more than 100.

Most cardinalfishes have a similar appearance, having a large mouth, large eyes, and two distinct dorsal fins, the first with only six to eight spines. Normally there are only two spines in the anal fin.

Most cardinalfishes, as the name implies, are colored red, although many species depart from this basic color and are variously colored. One, see figure 430, is distinctly patterned; it has a brassy gold head and red-spotted posterior, the two colors separated by a black band. The orbiculate cardinalfish, as it is called, spends more of its time out in the open in an aquarium than more secretive or shy species.

Cardinalfishes also are nocturnal animals, as the large eyes and general red color pattern would suggest.

Cardinalfishes usually occur on coral reefs or rocky areas where hiding places are abundant. They spend most of the bright hours of the day back in holes or under rocks, coming out at night to forage for food. There are exceptions to this generalization. Most are shallow-water fishes, with some species occurring in deeper water. And most are marine, although some prefer brackish or even fresh water.

Some of the cardinalfishes are very abundant, either in schools hovering over or very near the reef or as densely packed individuals, many fishes inhabiting a limited area.

The large mouth of most cardinalfishes usually denotes a predatory existence, small animals being dispatched with ease. The diet of the cardinalfishes consists of small fishes and invertebrates.

There is another use for the large mouth of cardinalfishes. Some are oral incubators, or, as such fishes are commonly called, mouthbrooders. The male is the usual holder of the eggs, although the female of some of the species tends the eggs. It is suspected that some species share the chores between male and female. At least some cardinalfishes build a nest and deposit the eggs therein. The eggs may be picked up by some males in times of danger, thus protecting the eggs. Is this perhaps the first step in the evolution of the mouthbrooding habit?

According to Dr. Earl Hearld, the brownspot cardinalfish, *Apogon uninotatus,* plays possum when cornered. This little cardinalfish is brownish, with a dark brown ocellated spot on its side, just above the pectoral fin.

Some cardinalfishes live commensally with certain molluscs. In the Caribbean Sea small species of the genus *Astrapogon* reside in the mantle cavity of the queen conch, *Strombus gigas,* or the bivalve *Pinna.*

The largest genus of cardinalfishes is *Apogon;* fishes of this genus are the most likely to be encountered. Another genus, *Siphamia,* contains small fishes (30-40 mm) with a silvery gland extending from the lower part of the head to near the caudal fin. This character is noticeable externally along the ventral side of the fish.

The cardinalfishes are generally good aquarium fishes, being hardy and colorful. There of course is the problem of their nocturnal habits, and for the first week or so cardinalfishes will be very secretive in an aquarium. Early in the morning or at evening the cardinalfish will make its appearence searching for bits of food.

Collecting cardinalfishes is usually not difficult once a little background information is known. If a collector is to be successful in capturing these fishes he must search the darker areas of the reef during the day. Most specimens are taken by lifting rather large rocks and scooping up the cardinalfish that are stunned by the bright light suddenly bursting upon them. Others can be chased into a cul-de-sac and trapped there.

428. *Apogon novemfasciatus* Cuvier & Valenciennes. 61 mm standard length. Western Samoa. Twin-spot cardinalfish. Photo by Dr. John E. Randall.

429. *Apogon robustus* (Smith & Radcliffe). Photo of a 3.1 inch specimen from the Palau Islands by Dr. John E. Randall.

430. *Apogon nematopterus* Bleeker. 30 mm standard length. Philippine Islands. Orbiculate cardinalfish.

431. *Apogon cyanosoma* Bleeker. 50 mm standard length. Okinawa. Gold-striped cardinalfish.

432. *Pempheris xanthoptera* Tominaga. Approximately 30 mm standard length. Moroiso, Kanagawa, Japan.

433. *Calloplesiops altivelis* (Steindachner). 120 mm standard length. Philippine Islands. Comet.

Family PEMPHERIDAE
SWEEPERS

Sweepers are small to moderate sized fishes found in tropical and temperate seas. The family consists of four genera, of which *Pempheris* is the largest.

Pempherids are rather unique-looking fishes, easily recognized. They have a small dorsal fin perched in the middle of the back and a long anal fin extending from the vent to the caudal peduncle. The body is compressed and usually deep for the typical form. The lateral line, or group of sense organs, extends high along the back. The eye is large, as is the mouth, which is very oblique.

Sweepers are said to be nocturnal fishes, which accounts for the large eyes. They also can be found in large schools around a reef. Like the cardinalfishes, they may be found in the darker regions of the reef such as under ledges or in caves.

The color patterns of the common sweepers are usually plain, without any distinctive markings. The colors themselves are subtle, ranging from coppery to pinkish, yellowish, or brown.

Pempheris oualensis of the Indo-Pacific region is one of the more common species. It is called the silver sweeper, even though the color is more brownish, with a silvery sheen. The leading edge of the dorsal fin and the base of the pectoral fin are darker brown. The silver sweeper is a schooling fish commonly found near the surface around shallow rocky areas or wrecks and piers. Some of the sweepers have been reported to be plankton feeders.

434. *Goniistius fuscus* Richardson. Adult. Great Barrier Reef, Australia. Red morwong. Photo by Dr. Herbert R. Axelrod.

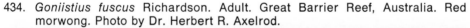

435. *Goniistius gibbosus* Richardson. Adult. Great Barrier Reef, Australia. Magpie morwong. Photo by Dr. Herbert R. Axelrod.

436. *Goniistius fuscus* Richardson. Adult. Great Barrier Reef, Australia. Red morwong. Photo by Dr. Herbert R. Axelrod.

437. *Goniistius zebra* (Döderlein). 150 mm standard length. Okinawa. Zebra morwong.

438. *Goniistius quadricornis* Günther. 200 mm standard length. Ito, Shizuoka, Japan. Barred morwong.

439. *Goniistius zonatus* (Cuvier & Valenciennes). 200 mm standard length. Moroiso, Kanagawa, Japan. Striped morwong.

440. *Priacanthus macracanthus* Cuvier. 200 mm standard length. Aburatsubo Marine Park, Japan. Bigeye.

441. *Goniistius zonatus* (Cuvier & Valenciennes). 40 mm standard length. Moroiso, Kanagawa, Japan. Juvenile striped morwong.

442. *Epinephelus coromandelicus* Day. 200 mm standard length. Aburatsubo Marine Park, Japan. Coromandel grouper.

A second genus can be distinguished by the extent of the lateral line. In *Pempheris* the lateral line reaches the end of the middle rays of the caudal fin; in *Parapriacanthus* the lateral line does not reach as far, extending only onto the basal third of the fin.

Family CHEILODACTYLIDAE
MORWONGS

The morwongs are often placed systematically in with the hawkfishes, family Cirrhitidae. The lower rays of the pectoral fins are unbranched and thickened much like the hawkfishes'. They often extend beyond the edge of the fin.

The body is somewhat elongate and covered with small or moderate scales. They have small mouths with thick lips and weak teeth, none on the roof of the mouth.

Morwongs are found in rather deep water, but strays are sometimes encountered in shallow water. They are good food fish and usually command a respectable price in the market.

The thickened pectoral rays are used as sensitive feelers when the fish forage for food around the rocky areas where they occur.

Two scientific names, *Cheilodactylus* and *Goniistius,* are generally applied to the commoner species of this family. The latter name is now gaining greater acceptance among ichthyologists.

Many of the species of the genus *Goniistius* are white with striking black bands, as can been seen in the accompanying photographs.

There is a considerable change in appearance between the juveniles and adults of these fishes. The young, according to Dr. J. L. B. Smith, have a highly compressed body, deep at the chest, with normal pectoral fins. The fins do not develop the thickened, extended rays until they are quite big.

Goniistius gibbosus, the magpie morwong, is an attractive species of this group. It grows to a size of about one foot and may be captured by hook and line or by commercial trawls.

The name morwong is the common name used in Australia for these fishes.

Family SERRANIDAE
GROUPERS

The groupers are a large and varied family of fishes with many subfamilies. Most of these subfamilies contain but a single genus of fishes, and many of these genera have but few species. This rather exceptional type of evolution seems to be attributed to the groupers' habit of not moving far from their homes, tempered with the fairly solitary existence to which most groupers subject themselves. Why should they be called "groupers" when they are better called "loners!"

As many divers will testify, groupers are rarely found in a group; they are more likely to be found as individual specimens in rocky caves. They are excellent fishes for the table, for hunting with a spear, and for the aquarium.

The two largest subfamilies of groupers are probably the Epinephelinae and Serraninae. The Epinephelinae is thus far the largest known subfamily, with six genera, including about 40 species, of which about 26 are found in the genus *Epinephelus* and 8 in the genus *Cephalopholis*. *Epinephelus moara* is an abundant Japanese grouper that is commonly eaten. A large specimen recently caught off Kochi was 134 cm long and weighed about 30 kg. Other specimens have been caught in Japan which weighed almost 90 kg. The Pacific contains the largest grouper in the world, and one of the largest teleost fishes, too, in the form of *E. damelii*. The Australian record for this fish is 180 cm and 360 kg.

Groupers spawn in pairs usually, and they spawn in the late spring. As the young hatch, they find their way to a shoreline where they hide among the floating eel grass or sea-weed. Groupers usually restrict their diets to living large crustaceans and fishes, and wherever they are found they are highly prized as food. Groupers are found in all the warm oceans of the world, but, of course, not the same species.

According to Dr. Leonard P. Schultz, "the color patterns of the groupers are of the utmost importance in distinguishing the various species, but not too much value should be placed on the presence or absence of the dark vertical bands; these appear to vary in intensity with age, more or less disappearing in adults of certain species. The dark blotches along the back, as well as the distribution of black spots elsewhere on the head and body, are very important characters." Certain groupers change dramatically as they grow. The young *Diploprion bifasciatus*, for example, has an extremely long filamentous dorsal ray several times longer than its body.

Unlike most members of the subfamily Epinephelinae, the ishi-nagi, *Stereolepis ishinagi* (Hilgendorf) prefers cold water and is found in areas where the air temperature often falls below freezing during several months of the year (such as Korea and Hokkaido). This is a food fish, of course, but many groupers are poisonous at times and may be the source of ciguatera poisoning. The cause of this poisonous condition in fishes has not yet been verified, but it is thought to be connected with the development of a poisonous alga which passes up through the food chain and becomes bio-magnified (a process similiar to "distillation" where a large fish eats a small fish and excretes everything it doesn't digest except the posion, which it stores in the fatty tissues of its body).

Two excellent aquarium groupers are *Aulacocephalus temmincki* Bleeker and *Chromileptes altivelis* (Cuvier & Valenciennes).

443. *Epinephelus coromandelicus* Day. 200 mm standard length. Aburatsubo Marine Park, Japan. Coromandel grouper.

444. *Epinephelus* sp. 200 mm standard length. Aburatsubo Marine Park, Japan.

445. *Epinephelus fario* (Thunberg). 350 mm standard length. Aburatsubo Marine Park, Japan. Spotted grouper.

446. *Epinephelus moara* (Temminck & Schlegel). 400 mm standard length. Aburatsubo Marine Park, Japan. Small fish are cleaner wrasses, *Labroides dimidiatus*.

447. *Epinephelus moara* (Temminck & Schlegel). 130 mm standard length. Aburatsubo, Kanagawa, Japan. Young.

448. *Cromileptes altivelis* (Cuvier & Valenciennes). 250 mm standard length. Okinawa. Polkadot grouper.

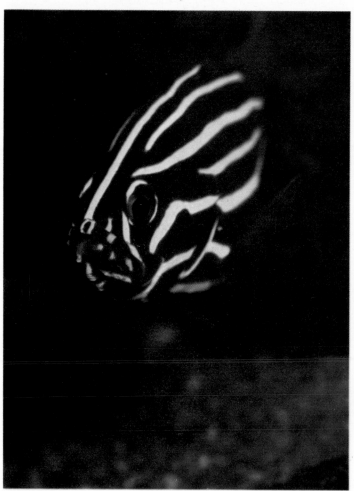

449. *Grammistes sexlineatus* (Thunberg). 180 mm standard length. Okinawa. Golden-striped grouper.

450. *Grammistes* sp. (possibly young of *G. sexlineatus*). 34 mm standard length. Eniwetok, Marshall Islands. Photo by Dr. John E. Randall.

The subfamily Grammistinae is closely related to the Epinephelinae. This subfamily contains some of the most beautiful . . . and most dangerous . . . of the groupers. *Grammistes sexlineatus* is probably two closely related subspecies which have been described as G. *s.sexlineatus* (Thunberg), and *G.s. proerythraeus* Fowler. The Fowler description is of a warmwater Ryukyu fish, while the Thunberg fish is from mainland Japan. The warmwater subspecies may at times be poisonous, exuding a slime which will kill everything in the aquarium, including itself! Take a good look at the figure of it so that you will be prepared should you happen to meet this fellow in a pet shop.

Grammistes sexlineatus

Perkins photo.

Family SCORPAENIDAE
SCORPIONFISHES

There is a very large group of fishes which have bony plates under their eyes. These fishes are called the mailed-cheek fishes and they include a large percentage of the living marine fishes of the Pacific, including the feared and poisonous turkey or lionfishes of the genera *Pterois* and *Dendrochirus (Brachirus)* and the dreaded stonefishes.

The systematic study of the scorpionfishes by Dr. L. P. Schultz indicated that the pectoral fin rays of certain scorpionfishes did not become fully branched until some individuals reached a length of 4 or 5 cm. In the aquarium trade, the discovery by fish collectors that some of the scorpionfishes are livebearers and that they are capable of having as many as 6,000 fry at one spawning, coupled with the fact that these fry are easily raised on newly hatched brine shrimp, flooded the market with small lionfishes.

The lionfishes and other scorpionfishes, especially small ones, may be interesting additions to the aquarium. Their usually large and beautiful pectoral fins, which spread wing-like, seem to be more of a hindrance in swimming than an asset. One fish behaviorist has even suggested that the lionfish uses its huge pectoral fins to corral or herd small fishes into its mouth. He obviously never saw a wild lionfish in action, as they lie in awkward positions on a reef, often with their heads pointed down. As a small fish comes near, with a fast, sudden spring the lionfish inhales, and the huge mouth conceals what was gobbled down. Only the slight movement of the jaws indicates the fate of the passerby.

In the aquarium some specimens may be interesting if they are kept with larger fishes. It is very true that they are poisonous, so don't handle them. The poison is primarily in their dorsal spines, but all their spiny rays may be poisonous . . . and they have spiny rays on their dorsal, pelvic and anal fins!

In the aquarium, they are best fed live fishes. If you live near a source of bait fish, offer them a few every few days; goldfish will serve nicely and survive long enough in salt water for the scorpionfish to get them.

Their poison may be potent even after the fishes are dead, so handle even the corpses of dead scorpionfishes with care.

Family ANTENNARIIDAE
ANGLERFISHES

Tide pools, coral reefs and beaches all provide safe ecological niches for the young of many species . . . so does a mass of floating seaweed. But in almost every large mass of seaweed you can find some surprises.

In some waters, seaweed is most plentiful from late winter through late spring. This just happens to coincide with the spawning season of many fishes, and the fry of these millions . . . or billions . . . of spawning fishes may end up hiding among the floating water weeds, drifting perhaps for thousands of miles as the winds and tides direct the destiny of everything that floats, including the seaweed in which the fry may be hiding. In this way many species get their world-wide distribution.

The most common of the floating seaweed is what is called "Sargassum weed," since it floats so thickly and is so conspicuous in the Sargasso Sea where the baby eels are produced. But Sargassum weed doesn't always float; sometimes it sinks, and when it does many of the baby fishes look for a new home . . . as they are just fishfood in the open waters.

Since these floating nurseries also serve as spawning grass for some fishes, it shouldn't be surprising that they may also serve as a hiding place for larger fishes, and Nature has made the incredibly odd-looking "Sargassum fish," *Histrio histrio,* which is almost totally invisible in Sargassum weed. Not only is there a Sargassum fish associated with the Sargassum weed, but there also is a group of fishes which are called "angler" fishes because their first spiny dorsal ray is modified into a fishing lure which the anglerfish holds in front of its mouth, hopefully attracting a small fish to go for the "bait." Instead the fish is inhaled down an ever-hungry gullet. This fish is always associated with floating seaweed. It never leaves the seaweed and rarely moves. All it does is lie in wait for a small fish. There are many other anglerfishes in the family Antennariidae, of which *Antennarius tridens, A. nox* and *A. sanguifluus* are the most popular in the aquarium trade.

Unlike *Histrio,* the *Antennarius* species do not lie among the seaweed, preferring to live on the bottom inside an old shoe or tire! Most anglerfishes are ugly and colorless, though some are bright red and yellow; they are not recommended for aquarium fishes, as they hardly ever move and they have no great interest for aquarists.

Text for families Muraenidae and Congridae appears on page 260; text for families Bothidae and Pleuronectidae begins on page 262.

Family MULLIDAE
GOATFISHES

Goatfishes have two separated dorsal fins, a small mouth, ventral in position (as is usual for bottom feeders), provided with small, conical teeth.

Goatfishes are well known for their long sensitive barbels which they use for locating food on the bottom sand. It is very interesting to watch a goatfish at work scouring the bottom with the flexible barbels. In an aquarium this action causes a problem by keeping the sediment stirred up.

Many of the goatfishes are red in color, often with black or yellow markings. Others are various shades of yellow or dark brown.

There are some fifty species of goatfishes known today, mostly in tropical waters. They average about one foot in length, although records of fishes twice that size are known. Goatfishes are inshore, relatively shallow-water fishes occurring either as individuals or in moderate-sized schools.

Larval goatfishes have been collected over deep water by night-light. They have the general shape of the goatfish but are silver in coloration. The barbels, not useful in open water, are tucked away, hiden from view. As soon as the barbels are found by the investigator, the identity of the fish as to family is certain.

Goatfishes have the ability to change colors from their normal pattern to a mottled pattern, perhaps as a protective device to help the fish "disappear" into the variegated background.

Common genera included in this family are *Mullus, Upeneus, Pseudupeneus,* and *Mulloidichthys.*

Goatfishes' food consists mainly of small crustaceans, worms, etc. Goatfishes themselves are used as food.

Family MONOCENTRIDAE
PINECONE FISHES

The Families MURAENIDAE And CONGRIDAE
MORAY AND CONGER EELS

The pinecone fishes are very peculiar fishes; their scales are modified into plate-like armor resembling the pine cones for which they were named.

There are only two species of pinecone fishes known, one from the coasts of Australia, the other from the Indo-Pacific.

The pinecone fish found in the area around Japan, *Monocentris japonicus,* reaches a length of about 5 inches. It is found in relatively deep water and usually in schools. This species is not common, and when it is displayed in public aquariums it draws a great deal of attention. In Japan it is a food fish and is prepared in several different ways, including soya bean soup.

The Australian species, *Monocentris gloriaemaris,* has been collected by commercial trawlers off Queensland; dried specimens sometimes turn up on the beaches after a storm. The species is quite colorful, being basically yellow but with markings of black, orange, white, and red.

Both species are said to possess light organs which produce light by means of the symbiotic phosphorescent bacteria. The organs are located under the chin of these fishes. The lights of the Australian species have earned it its common name of "port and starboard light fish."

The pinecone fishes are very spiny, with the fins being no exception. The pelvic fin spine is quite prominent, as are the dorsal fin spines. Another peculiarity of the dorsal fin spines is that they are not in alignment. The first spine is inclined to one side, the second spine to the other, etc.

The food of the pinecone fish is not known. Is it possible that the light organs are instrumental in attracting or searching out the possible food items?

It is not difficult to associate the "moray" eels with the family Muraenidae and the "conger" eels with the family Congridae, as these common epithets are similar to the scientific family names.

The various tropical waters of the Pacific almost universally harbor eels which lie rather surreptitiously amongst the rocks and coral crevices and heavy thickets of seaweed. While many of the eels are "snake-like," they have no close relationship with the sea snakes, even though many moray eels may be seen chasing crabs across exposed coral heads or beaches.

The two families presented here are included in the sub-order Anguillina of the order Apodes, which characteristically metamorphose through a transparent, leaf-shaped larval stage known as a "leptocephalus." During early spring, certain coastlines swarm with the leptocephali of many species of conger eels; the leptocephali of the moray eels, like their parents, rarely leave the bottom of the warm ocean.

Several aquarists and scientists have collected various eel leptocephali and raised them in aquariums (only recently did a Japanese scientist, Dr. Toshio Ishii, spawn a coldwater eel, *Anguilla,* in an aquarium after the eels had been injected in the dorsal musculature with Synahorin, diethylstilbestrol, homogenized pituitary gland of rainbow trout oralphatocopherol). As the leptocephali grow, they become shorter and thicker in proportion, and their transparent body becomes opaque. The origin of the dorsal fin and the position of the anal pore move forward until the metamorphosis is

451. *Epinephelus
kohleri* Schultz.
400 mm standard
length. Ueno Zoo
Aquarium, Japan.
Kohler's
grouper.

452. *Epinephelus
merra* Bloch. 200
mm standard
length. Ogasawara
Islands, Japan.

453. *Epinephelus
cometae* Tanaka.
200 mm standard
length. Shimoda,
Shizuoka, Japan.
Comet grouper.

complete, at which time the fish begins to look like an eel and drops to the bottom, where it takes up its familiar life style.

Congers, morays and snake eels, while having their eel-like appearance in common, can readily be distinguished. The morays lack both pectoral and pelvic fins, while the congers and snake eels lack only their pelvics.

The aquarium is not the usual place for a colony of eels, though almost every public aquarium in the world has some on display. Moray eels are probably the most common aquarium eels, and as long as they have plenty to eat, enough room, and a suitable hiding place, they seem to do very well. In nature morays feed upon crabs and octopuses. Most aquarists know better than to keep octopuses with morays, for they almost always engage in a fight to the death . . . with the octopus being the one that usually ends up dead!

Most eels, especially the morays, are ugly, irregularly colored and dangerous to handle. If speared, they may slide down the spear and bite their tormentor. The author prefers to leave them alone . . .both in the aquarium and in their niche in the reef.

Family BOTHIDAE
LEFT-EYED FLOUNDERS

Flounders are peculiar fishes in which both eyes are on one side of the head. In the case of the family Bothidae, the eyes are found on the left side; hence the fishes are referred to as the left-eye flounders.

The eyes of all flounders start off normally positioned in the larvae. With age, one of the eyes migrates to the same side of the head as the other eye at about the time the fish is ready to settle. When the fish takes up the bottom type existence, the eyes are then both directed upwards rather than having one eye uselessly facing the substrate.

Although distinctly flattened, the left-eye flounders can accommodate rather large pieces of food with their large mouths. They are quick to engulf the small fishes and crustaceans that make up their diet. To accomplish the capture of their prey the flounders are adept at adopting the color and pattern of the background, within reason of course. This camouflage is aided by the sand the fish works onto its fins and back as it partially buries itself.

Generally included in the bothids or left-eye flounders are the genera *Arnoglossus, Lophonectes, Bothus, Pelecanichthys,* etc.

Family PLEURONECTIDAE
RIGHT-EYED FLOUNDERS

As their common name indicates, fishes of this family differ from the Bothidae in having the eyes on the right side of the head, the left side being the eyeless side on the bottom. The flounders are greatly compressed; that is, they are flattened from side to side, rather than depressed or flattened from top to bottom. They therefore lie on their sides, not on the ventral part of their body like depressed fishes.

The eggs of the right-eye flounders are pelagic, as are those of the left-eye flounders, but lack the conspicuous oil globule that is present in the eggs of the left-eye flounders. Development proceeds much like that of other flounders in that the larvae are bilaterally symmetrical, with one eye on each side of the head.

Most flounders are marine coastal fishes occurring on mud or sand bottoms. Great numbers of these fishes are trawled yearly for human consumption. This family includes some of the more famous food fishes like the plaice, turbot, and halibut.

In some cases there is a reversal in the direction of migration of the eyes, resulting in flounders with eyes "on the wrong side of the head."

Though the majority of right-eye flounders are strictly marine species, some are able to enter brackish or even fresh water. For example, the starry flounder, *Platichthys stellatus,* can be found in estuaries and certain lakes and rivers of Japan.

Additional characteristics used to distinguish the right-eye flounders are that in them the right ventral fin is larger in size and has more rays than the left one, and the right pectoral fin usually is larger than the left.

The right-eye flounders are often called the right-handed flounders. Their diet consists of small fishes as well as crustaceans and other invertebrate animals.

454. *Pterois antennata* Bloch. Attains a length of 200 mm. Indo-Pacific region including the Red Sea. Spotfin lionfish. Photo by Dr. D. Terver of the Nancy Aquarium, France.

455. *Pterois lunulata* Temminck & Schlegel. 200 mm standard length. Aburatsubo Marine Park, Japan. Notice the resemblance between this species and *Pterois volitans* (figure 457).

456. *Pterois antennata* Bloch. 80 mm standard length. Okinawa. Zebra lionfish. Although resembling the true lionfish (genus *Pterois*) this fish is placed in a separate genus.

457. *Pterois volitans* (Linnaeus). 120 mm standard length. Okinawa. Turkey fish. This species is probably the most poisonous of the lionfishes (genus *Pterois*).

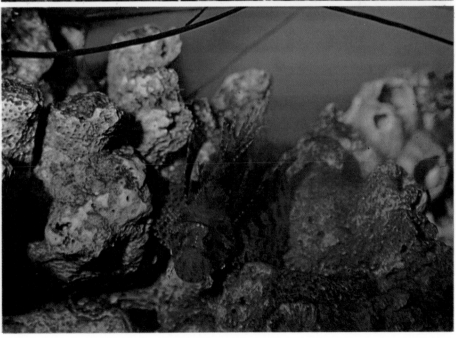

458. *Dendrochirus* sp. 60 mm standard length. Okinawa.

459. Unidentified juvenile scorpionfish. 15 mm standard length. Shimoda, Shizuoka, Japan.

460. *Sebasticus marmoratus* Cuvier & Valenciennes. 60 mm standard length. Shimoda, Shizuoka, Japan.

461. Unidentified juvenile scorpionfish about 50 mm standard length. Okinawa.

462. *Sebasticus marmoratus* Cuvier & Valenciennes. Adult. (No collection data available).

463. *Helicolenus hilgendorfi* (Steindachner & Döderlein). 150 mm. Ito, Shizuoka, Japan.

464. *Scorpaena neglecta* Temminck & Schlegel. 150 mm. Aburatsubo, Kanagawa, Japan.

465. *Scorpaenopsis cirrhosa* (Thunberg). 150 mm. Ito, Shizuoka, Japan.

466. *Inimicus didactylum* (Pallas). (No data available). Indo-Pacific. Popeyed sea goblin.

467. Unidentified scorpionfish about 130 mm standard length. Aburatsubo, Kanagawa, Japan.

468. *Antennarius tridens* (Temminck & Schlegel). 60 mm standard length.

469. *Scorpaena neglecta* (Temminck & Schlegel). Ito, Shizuoka, Japan.

470. *Inimicus didactylum* (Pallas). 180 mm standard length. Enoshima Aquarium, Japan.

471. *Plotosus anguillaris* (Bloch). 100 mm standard length. Aburatsubo, Kanagawa, Japan. Striped catfish.

472. *Plotosus anguillaris* (Bloch). 100 mm standard length. Aburatsubo, Kanagawa, Japan. Close up of head.

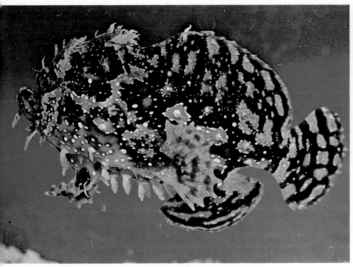

473. *Histrio histrio* (Linnaeus). 50 mm standard length. Sargassum fish.

474. *Histrio histrio* (Linnaeus). 50 mm standard length. Sargassum fish.

475. *Upeneus bensasi*
(Temminck &
Schlegel). 50 mm
standard length.
Aburatsubo, Kanagawa,
Japan. Salmonet.

476. *Parupeneus trifasciatus*
(Lacépède). 40 mm
standard length.
Okinawa.

478. *Upeneus bensasi* (Tem-
minck & Schlegel). 50 mm.
Aburatsubo, Kanagawa,
Japan.

477. *Parupeneus barberinoides* (Bleeker). 30 mm standard length. Okinawa.
Half-and-half goatfish.

479. *Monocentris japonicus* (Houttuyn). 50 mm standard length. Aburatsubo Marine Park, Japan. Pinecone fish.

480. *Monocentris japonicus* (Houttuyn). 20 mm standard length. Shimoda, Shizuoka, Japan. Pinecone fish (juvenile).

481. *Arctoscopus japonicus* Steindachner. 180 mm standard length. Enoshima Aquarium, Japan.

482. *Gymnothorax kidako* (Temminck & Schlegel). Adult. Ito, Shizuoka, Japan.

483. Underwater photograph of a moray eel, probably genus *Gymnothorax*.

484. *Gymnothorax leucostigma* Jordan & Richardson. Adult. Aburatsubo Marine Park, Japan.

485. *Rhinomuraena amboinensis* Barbour. Adults. Philippine Islands. Blue ribbon eel.

486. *Rhinomuraena quaesita* Garman. Adult. Aburatsubo Marine Park, Japan (possibly imported from the Philippine Islands). Black ribbon eel.

487. *Astroconger myriaster* (Brevoort). Tokyo University Aquarium, Misaki, Kanagawa, Japan. Japanese conger eel.

488. *Pseudorhombus cinnamoneus* (Temminck & Schlegel). 150 mm standard length. Izu Marine Park, Japan. Cinnamon flounder.

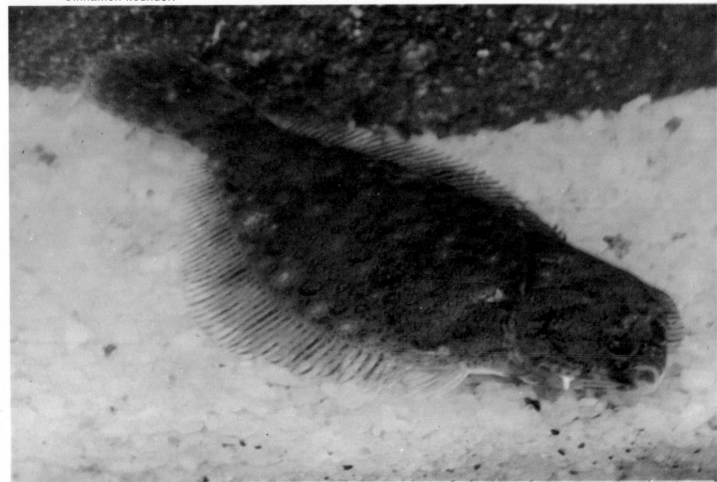

489. *Eopsetta grigorjewi* (Herzenstein). 40 mm standard length. Aburatsubo, Kanagawa, Japan. Spotted halibut.

INDEX

Page numbers in **bold** face refer to illustrations